THE LIFE AND MESSAGE OF

SISTER MARY

OF THE HOLY TRINITY

POOR CLARE OF JERUSALEM
(1901-1942)

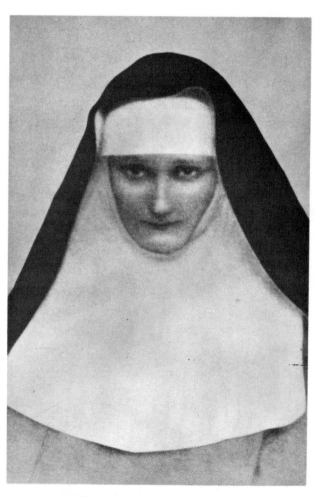

SISTER MARY OF THE TRINITY

THE LIFE AND MESSAGE OF

SISTER MARY
OF THE HOLY TRINITY

POOR CLARE OF JERUSALEM
(1901-1942)

by

Father Alain-Marie Duboin, O.F.M.

Translated by
Mary Douglas Chomeau

Revised and edited by
The Poor Clares of Rockford, Illinois

and

Raphael Brown, S.F.O.

Published in cooperation with the
Poor Clares Corpus Christi Monastery,
Rockford, Illinois.

TAN BOOKS AND PUBLISHERS, INC.
Rockford, Illinois 61105

Anyone obtaining favors through the intercession of Sister Mary of the Trinity or wishing to know more about the enclosed contemplative vocation of the Poor Clares as lived today may write to The Poor Clares, Corpus Christi Monastery, 2111 South Main Street, Rockford, Illinois 61102.

TAN BOOKS AND PUBLISHERS, INC.
P.O. Box 424
Rockford, Illinois 61105

1987

DECLARATION OF OBEDIENCE

In complete submission to the Holy Roman Catholic Church, and in conformity with the decrees of Pope Urban VIII, we declare that we have no wish to anticipate in any way the judgment of the Church on the nature of the communications made to Sister Mary of the Trinity, or to attribute to the words contained in this work any other meaning than that which the above-mentioned decrees permit.

—The Editors

CONTENTS

Introduction
by Raphael Brown ix
Author's Note
by Father Duboin xiii

— Part One —
THE LIFE

1. Childhood and Youth (1901-1926)
   by Father Duboin 3
2. Conversion and Vocation (1926-1938)
   *by Father van den Broek and
   the Poor Clares of Rockford* 34
3. In the Harbor: Poor Clare in Jerusalem (1938-1942)
   *by Father Duboin and
   the Poor Clares of Rockford* 74
4. Last Days (1942)
   *by Father Duboin and
   the Poor Clares of Rockford* 126

— Part Two —
THE MESSAGE

Introduction
by Father Duboin 137
1. The Message and the Messenger
   *by Father van den Broek, Father Duboin, and
   the Poor Clares of Rockford* 142
2. The Vow of Victim
   by Father Duboin 150
3. Words of Our Lord to Sister Mary of the Trinity
   selected by Sister Mary Gabriel, P.C. 158
4. Living the Gospel Life—More Words of Our Lord
   selected by the Poor Clares of Rockford 183
5. Prayers of Sister Mary of the Trinity
   selected by the Poor Clares of Rockford 217
6. Epilogue and Bibliography: Franciscan Connections
   by Raphael Brown 225

Appendix: "Hidden Goodness: Rockford's Poor Clares"
   Chicago Tribune article by Robert McClory ..240

INTRODUCTION
by Raphael Brown

Sister Mary of the Trinity (1901-1942) was the daughter of a French Swiss Protestant missionary in South Africa who became a Catholic in Italy and a Poor Clare in Jerusalem. There during the last years of her life she recorded 665 "Notes," which consist of words seemingly spoken by Jesus Christ. Those Notes, along with autobiographical material by Sister Mary entitled "Conversion and Vocation," were published by her Belgian Franciscan spiritual director in Beirut in 1943 and in Belgium in 1947.

An English translation of this work by a British Poor Clare and myself was published by the Newman Press and by Mercier Press in Ireland in 1950. The Newman Press edition, *The Spiritual Legacy of Sister Mary of the Holy Trinity,* was reprinted in 1981 by TAN Books and Publishers, in cooperation with the Poor Clares of Rockford, Illinois.

Meanwhile, in 1979, another French edition of the "Notes," with important new materials on Sister Mary's life, edited by the French Swiss Franciscan Father Alain Duboin, was published in Paris by Apostolat des Editions and in Montreal by Editions Paulines. The Rockford Poor Clares have undertaken to bring out in English the new data in that book. (That French work also included most of the Sister's Notes, all of which are already available in English as *The Spiritual Legacy of Sister Mary of the Holy Trinity.*) Only certain selections from the Notes, arranged by topic, are given in this present volume.

I will now describe the important new materials which appear for the first time in English in this present work.

In *Part One: The Life,* the chapter entitled "Childhood and Youth" was written by Father Duboin using an unpublished manuscript by her spiritual director in Jerusalem, the Belgian Franciscan Father Silvère van den Broek, who died in 1949. Father Duboin added to that text and used in other parts of his book new biographical information obtained from interviews and letters written by the Sister.

He also inserted that information in the form of footnotes in the account of her "Conversion and Vocation" and throughout the 200 pages of her Notes. As both the Notes and "Conversion and Vocation" (of course without his footnotes) are available in the 1981 TAN Books reprinting of *The Spiritual Legacy of Sister Mary of the Holy Trinity,* we have had to find another way to present all the new material.

We have therefore decided that three new biographical chapters would be composed by the Poor Clares of Rockford, blending footnotes from *The Spiritual Legacy* in with Father Duboin's versions to produce a flowing narrative. This material makes up Chapters 2, 3 and 4 of Part One: "Conversion and Vocation," "In the Harbor," and "Last Days." (The first is based on Sister Mary's own account and includes information given in the section entitled "Conversion and Vocation" in *Spiritual Legacy.*)

Part Two: The Message contains Father Duboin's *Introduction* to the Notes, supplemented by an essay entitled "The Message and the Messenger" by the Poor Clares of Rockford. (I decided to condense

Father Duboin's text in the light of a background letter which he wrote to me in December of 1979.)

Next we present three groups of extracts from Sister Mary of the Trinity's Notes arranged by topic; these were selected by Sister Mary Gabriel and the Poor Clares of Rockford. Here we have included Father Duboin's "Summary" of the Vow of Victim, with appropriate extracts from the Notes. The Rockford Sisters have added a selection of Prayers written by or loved by their Sister.

I have appended an *Epilogue* entitled "Franciscan Connections," which contains biographical information about the editors and translators of the Belgian, French and American editions, with data about related persons and projects.

Then, after the *Epilogue,* the book ends with a relevant *Appendix:* "Hidden Goodness," a readable *Chicago Tribune* article by Robert McClory on the way of life and spirituality of the Poor Clares of Rockford, Illinois, with a profile of their abbess, Mother Mary Dorothy—to whose zeal we owe this book on Sister Mary of the Trinity.

This book also contains a number of illustrations which Father Duboin obtained and reproduced in his work. All the materials in that book which have been used in this one are published by authorization of Apostolat de Editions (now renamed Mediaspaul Editions).

At the end of this project, which has extended over several years, this editor wishes to express his warm gratitude to all who have patiently and persistently collaborated in it. May God richly bless and reward each and all!

—Raphael Brown

NOTE

The word "Holy" was added to Sister Mary of the Trinity's name in the 1950 and 1981 English editions of *The Spiritual Legacy of Sister Mary of the Holy Trinity.* However, as that word was not used in her signature or in the French editions of her writings, it has been omitted in this book, except—for identification—in the title and in references to *The Spiritual Legacy of Sister Mary of the Holy Trinity.*

As this book forms a supplement to that one, readers should also have and make use of *The Spiritual Legacy.*

—The Editors

AUTHOR'S NOTE

(This Author's Note was originally written for Father Duboin's book entitled Qu'un meme amour nous rassemble.*)*

This book owes almost everything to the work of the Reverend Father Silvère van den Broek, a Belgian Franciscan, chaplain of the Poor Clares of Jerusalem and first editor of the writings of Sister Mary of the Trinity.[1]

Father Silvère died at Malines on February 11, 1949, while he was working on a biography of the Sister. He left an extensive collection of correspondence between the Sister and her family and friends, as well as some testimonial documents which he had assembled. Through the courtesy of the Friars Minor of the Province of St. Joseph in Belgium, we have been able to make use of those documents, and we have supplemented them by personal research in order to write the biographical sections of this book and to update and renew the footnotes to the Sister's writings.

—Father Alain-Marie Duboin, O.F.M.

---

[1] *Soeur Marie de la Trinite—Louisa Jaques, Clarisse de Jerusalem (1901-1942).*

First edition: Beirut 1943.

Second edition: Malines 1947-48.

That work has also been published in English, German, Italian, and Flemish.

— Part One —

THE LIFE

Que ta _paix_, Seigneur, et ta
tranquillité, ta charité et ta grâce, la
miséricorde de ta divinité soient
avec nous et parmi nous; tous les
jours de notre vie, maintenant, en
tout temps, et jusqu'aux siècles
des siècles —   Amen

Prière Syriaque — IVᵉ siècle.

CHILDHOOD AND YOUTH
(1901 - 1926)

Louisa Jaques was born in Pretoria, in the Transvaal, South Africa, on April 26, 1901. Her father, Numa Jaques, was a Protestant minister. With his wife, he ran a post of the "Swiss Mission." Both of them originally came from the Jura mountains in the canton of Vaud, Switzerland.

The mountains and forests of their birthplace had forged their characters. The Jura is an austere region, winter there is long and rough, and the population is hard-working. To supplement the insufficient income from agriculture, a local industry had been born generations before. Shops, or little factories, produced pieces for clock-making and precision machines. Hence the natives of the Jura acquired an acute sense of exact and minute work and a lofty professional conscience.

The Protestant Reformation, imposed on the region by the victory of Bern, found there favorable ground to welcome the strictest Calvinist doctrine. The liberal tendencies of the 19th century scarcely took hold on these parishes. Rather, the faithful turned toward movements of religious awakening or toward sects in order to defend their faith and maintain a demanding morality. Their mentality remained very distant from the Catholic religion.

3

At the time he was a young worker in a factory at L'Auberson, Louisa's father felt the missionary vocation well up in him while he was listening to a sermon. It was an irresistible call. Fighting opposition from many sides, he had to earn the money necessary for his preparatory studies. No obstacle stopped him, and he successfully finished his missionary formation at Lausanne.

His wife-to-be, whose maiden name was Elisa Bornand, showed the same aims of apostleship. With ardent piety, she rose early every morning to read the Bible and to pray. She became engaged to Mr. Jaques soon after his return from Lausanne, but refused to marry him before being certain they would be able to go to the missions. The French-speaking mission to which her fiance belonged was, in fact, slow in assigning to him the post where he was to exercise his ministry.

After the oldest child, Alexander, then two daughters, Elizabeth and Alice, Louisa was the fourth child in this household. More than the others, she inherited her mother's character: determined and energetic, firm in her principles.

Her birth, alas, did not bring all the joy that they had anticipated. The Boer War was going on and the country was enduring a period of alarming drought. The double burden of the Mission and the family was heavy. The arrival of a girl disappointed the parents who had hoped for a boy. Madame Jaques had dreamt of a son with a tempered character who would have a brilliant career. A few hours after Louisa's birth, this courageous mother was carried off by a sudden illness. She was 36. Before dying, she took the newborn child in her arms and said,

"We will love her dearly just the same."

Later, during the stay in the Transvaal, when Louisa inquired about her mother among some old blacks, the family's servants, her joy was great on hearing that they remembered her mother's piety: she was "the woman who prayed." The death of Madame Jaques so soon after the birth of the child deprived the latter of maternal tenderness. At the same time, this catastrophe plunged the father into dismay. The baby, scarcely arrived in the world, suffered from involuntary abandonment. Illness struck other members of the Mission. All their efforts were aimed at driving death away, and they forgot to welcome the life which had just blossomed out.

Soon, however, overcoming his grief, the father carried over to the little Louisa the affection he had had for his spouse. From then on, she was the object of a special attachment.

After the death of Louisa in Jerusalem, Mr. Jaques wrote to the Mother Abbess that the child had been offered to God even before her birth.

Providence watched over the little orphan. Her Aunt Alice, who had helped Madame Jaques on her deathbed, had been living in the house for nearly two years. A cultivated person, she had spent several years in England as assistant directress of a boarding school for girls. She had planned to go back to Switzerland and open her own boarding school with a friend, but before that, she had wanted to visit her sister in Africa. She arrived there just in time to be godmother of the third child, a girl to whom they gave the name of Alice. The war obliged her to prolong her stay, and after the death of her sister, she generously devoted her time to raising the orphans.

In 1902, with the war over, Mr. Jaques resolved to take his children to Switzerland, hoping to improve their health. During the siege of Pretoria, they had suffered from malnutrition; Louisa's health was particularly affected. They left Pretoria on June 4, 1902, and arrived in Switzerland in the beginning of July. Aunt Alice, whom the children would call their "Little Mother" henceforth, was with them. The family settled first in L'Auberson, at the house of the maternal grandmother. At the end of autumn in 1903, they moved to Morges on the shore of Lake Leman (or Lake of Geneva).

On May 1, 1904, his holiday ended, Mr. Jaques went back to his Mission, bringing with him his oldest child, Alexander. Aunt Alice, giving up her plans for a boarding school, devoted herself, along with her younger sister, Rosa, to raising the motherless girls.

Years later, after the death of Sister Mary of the Trinity, her sister Alice frankly admitted: "I wonder if some blame didn't weigh on Louisa's childhood. It is true that age is without pity! And I would believe that perhaps we, her older siblings, had the cruelty to reproach her for her sad coming into the world. Louisa was born during the passage of a comet. We had the habit of reminding her that the little Negroes who were born the same day as she had been thrown to the crocodiles. It seems to me that her birthdays, on April 26, were celebrated with a mixture of sadness."

The sight of the coffin next to the cradle had overshadowed the dawn of this life.

"Little Louisa is a very good baby who scarcely ever cries, either day or night," Aunt Alice noted in 1902 when the family settled in Switzerland. The child was surrounded with all possible care. In spite of that, her frail constitution suffered from the Swiss climate. The very first winter, she contracted pleurisy from which she kept a stubborn cough and chronic bronchitis. Several times during her childhood, she had pulmonary congestion. All that in spite of the attentive care of "Little Mother," who dressed her in woolens in every season and, for fear of her getting a chill, did not permit her to go play outside with the other children. Louisa's sprightly and lively nature suffered greatly from this constant privation of the pleasures given her older sisters.

She became a very alert little girl with decided gestures. With her observing looks, she followed all the gestures of her sisters, their attitudes, their movements, without imitating them, however. The independence of her character was manifesting itself already.

Her sister Alice, who would always remain the closest to Louisa, gave this testimony about her: "Louisa always had a good and generous character. While she was still a child, we already considered her the angel of the family... Although she was younger, I always felt that she was superior to me. It is as if, while still little, she knew how to read the souls of people. Therefore, 'Little Mother,' who was not perfect, feared Louisa a little. Although she was very sensitive, Louisa did not cry easily. I remember seeing her cry only a few times, but how much more concentrated were the tears which flowed then."

Between the two aunts, there was 15 years difference. Rosa, the younger, sometimes suffered from the
authoritarianism of her older sister. The good heart
of Louisa understood, and she showed Rosa more
affection than did any of her other sisters, trying
in this fashion to make her life more agreeable.

Aunt Alice devoted an attentive solicitude to the
religious formation of her nieces. During her entire
childhood, Louisa faithfully recited her prayers each
evening, no matter what the hour at which the children went to bed and despite the somewhat annoyed
reproaches of her older sisters.

Aunt Alice's religious discipline was severe. Each
day, at the end of the meal, the children had a family ritual of prayers and readings. One day, a young
cousin was at the house. She was four years old and
Louisa was 14. Finding the time dragging, the child
covered her nose with some tin foil and was having
fun peeping over it. Louisa could not stifle an out-
burst of laughter, which amused her sisters: everyone broke out laughing. Indignant, Aunt Alice
ordered Louisa to leave the table and go outside.

In good years as in bad, the two aunts with the
children went up to L'Auberson, to the old home of
their grandparents for the summer vacation. One
Sunday morning, the three little girls were at church
with "Little Mother" in their habitual place, the
third pew from the front on the left side of the nave.
Suddenly Aunt Alice was distracted from the sermon by the appearance of Louisa, who, red enough
to burst, seemed on the point of smothering. She
hurried to take her by the hand and to leave the
church with her. The poor child—she was not yet
10 years old—was holding herself back with all her

might. She did not dare cough in church!

Very soon, Louisa learned to be of service and to devote herself to others. When there were errands to run, "Little Mother" told the oldest girl to do it. The latter passed the errand on to the second one, who foisted it off on the youngest. Louisa performed it with good humor. For her, to be of service was the most natural thing in the world. She did not know what it was to pout. "Louisa," wrote her sister Alice, "didn't know what bad humor was, neither as a child nor later. Bad humor makes others suffer. Louisa never did that."

Close-mouthed and meditative, Louisa manifested from childhood a profound aspiration for the beautiful, the perfect. This desire for perfection, always unsatisfied, was shown in the thoughtfulness of her behavior, in the affability of her manners. She suffered from not being able to communicate better this need, to have this desire shared. Therefore she often felt misunderstood and isolated.

Absentmindedness was her principal fault. She grieved over it during her entire life. Must we explain it by her isolation? "She was often distracted," noted her sister Alice, "absorbed in her reflections and completely absent from what was going on around her."

With Louisa, "Little Mother" found again her vocation as a teacher. While watching over the ever-precarious health of her niece, she taught her to read and prepared her for life at school with more success than with the older sisters. It is true that a lesson given by Aunt Alice demanded fixed immobility and unfailing attention. The lack of discipline of the older sisters had worn down her patience.

While Louisa showed herself to be more studious, she also occasionally wanted to play truant. One day, she hid her alphabet and primer books. Neither the reasoned lectures of "Little Mother" nor the fruitless searches of her sisters under the furniture succeeded in shaking her resolve. She remained imperturbable in her decision to take a vacation that day.

As soon as she knew how to talk, Louisa related to her older sisters stories which she made up. "Little Mother" gave her a thick notebook covered with black artcloth to write down all her tales. Louisa accomplished this task with joy; she took great care in keeping this notebook. At that time, she was between five and six years old. Not knowing how to spell, she wrote phonetically. All of it was her own invention; neither collaboration nor advice were given her. She illustrated the stories with pictures cut from the newspaper; adventures where the people, animals and flowers spoke equally. Each story ended with a little moral in the fashion of La Fontaine's fables. This collection was the joy of her sisters. They browsed through the stories in order to read the conclusions, which always greatly amused them.

As soon as she entered school, Louisa set aside her notebook of stories once and for all. Well prepared by her aunt, she made rapid progress in school.

She completed the several stages of education in private institutions. The college which she went to could only give a private degree. Later she had to go to a state teacher's college in order to obtain the certificate required for teaching in parish schools.

In Switzerland, neutral and protected, the declaration of war in 1914 scarcely troubled the Jaques family living in Morges. They reckoned with the sufferings in neighboring countries, which they tried to alleviate by participating in projects to assist prisoners and the seriously wounded.

In February, 1915, Louisa experienced her first great sorrow.

She lost her music teacher, who died suddenly at the age of 36 after an apparently minor operation. Louisa felt a strong admiration for this woman, to whom she had become profoundly attached, and who also admired her. The tragic news was announced too brusquely by a visitor. Louisa remained silent with grief, then she ran into her bedroom and, on her knees in front of her bed, sobbed for a long time, her head under the covers. She kept as a treasure a gift that the teacher had made to her: a little book of religious thoughts which she read every evening, without fail, before going to sleep.

Not long before the war, her brother, Alexander, the oldest child of the family, had come back from Africa to study theology at Lausanne. The three sisters and their brother spent their summer vacations together in L'Auberson. In 1916, they took advantage of particularly favorable weather to make numerous trips in the mountains. The fatigue was too much for Louisa, who developed a fever. At the end of vacation time, they kept her at L'Auberson until she regained her health. She returned to Morges in November for her last year of courses and obtained her diploma in the beginning of the summer of 1917. Louisa planned to study at the university, and with this purpose in mind, began to prepare for the federal entrance examination. Her family opposed the idea, however, because of her frail health. This was a great sacrifice for Louisa, but the thirst for learning did not abandon her.

Vacation time that year was clouded by another trial, the death of Aunt Rosa. More reserved than her older sister, very devoted, very pious, too—she belonged to the Salvation Army—with her presence she tempered the austerity of family life. Aunt Rosa died prematurely after months of painful struggling against the cancer that finally carried her off.

After a few weeks of rest at L'Auberson, Louisa went back to Morges. There she found her first job. She was engaged as a private secretary by an old gentleman from Lausanne. She stayed there only a short time. Before winter came, she met Mr. and Mrs. Horber, both from Lausanne, too, but residing then in Adelboden in the Alps near Bern. They were working on starting a "League for Post-War Reforms," which indeed was founded a year later. They offered Louisa a job as a French-speaking secretary. That position had many aspects which pleased her, including working for a good cause by helping generous philanthropists. In their chalet at Adelboden, the Horbers gathered as many orphans as the house would shelter. They engaged several teachers to take care of these children, providing for their upkeep and education.

In their home, Louisa was the favorite child of the house. They had offered her this job in the hope that the mountain air would fortify her shaken health. On her side, she tried to be as much of service as possible, and she was very much appreciated right away. But in spite of her enthusiasm for her job, she felt the isolation. Louisa needed, she would always need, the affection of her relatives. So she wrote letters. From this period date a good number of letters, addressed for the most part to her sister Alice, others to faithful friends. If these letters have been preserved, it is not only through family affection or fidelity in friendship; they are never banal.

Through the events, Louisa shows her heart and soul. She relates her impressions of her first contacts with the world. Her personality is sketched in the letters very clearly, as one finds it in the story of her conversion or in her notebooks. One discerns a lively intelligence, profound sensitivity, a rare nobility of sentiments: she does not admit that one should make any compromise with one's conscience. Always courageous, she keeps quiet about her own concerns, her disappointments; she wants to think of others first, to bring them joy and light.

Her letters attest to a quest for the absolute. Louisa tried to get to the bottom of things, to give her life the fullest meaning possible.

"Your large packet of letters gave me immense pleasure..." It was July 14, 1918. Since the end of the preceding year, Louisa had been the secretary in the home of Dr. Horber and his wife. A month before, she had joined them in the chalet at Adelboden. She had just received letters from her whole family, transmitted by her sister Alice, and she hastened to reply.

"I came here in complete disarray; I have neglected my affairs; Mr. and Mrs. H. asked me to put my things in order first. Therefore, during a whole week, I worked for myself, without losing a minute. I am going to work hard now and especially work on myself. The other work is only a reflection of this first inner work. That is something Mr. H. taught me; before, I tried only to help others and did not concern myself with myself. Now, I know that it is nothing to be useful in many things; one must *become* something oneself. That is the only way which produces results, and one becomes something by approaching God, by approaching Christ, who communicates His strength to us; it is something that one cannot explain. It seems to me that I have learned how to pray here. After praying, I feel so strong, while before I was so weak. I feel incapable, but I know the means of becoming strong, true strength which can do everything; one receives it only from on high in the measure that one asks for it, that one waits for it. I have to grow; pray for me."

These words from a girl of 17, these generous resolutions, indicated a good start in life, the promise of a magnificent springtime. But this beautiful impulse would be shattered—and so often. Interrupted, but not destroyed, it would always start over from the most profound depths of her being, more mature, more solid, until the time would come to bear fruit.

In the same letter, she spoke of her health which, she assured, could not be better. However, a few weeks later, she joined her sisters at L'Auberson for a vacation and could do no more than the previous year to take part in the trips in the mountains. The doctor who was consulted found a marked anemia.

She was told to rest and be prudent. People were

beginning to talk of the terrible flu of 1918; there had already been some deaths.

In September, Louisa went back to work at the home of the Horbers, who meanwhile returned to Lausanne. Still tired, she had to see the doctor. The woman doctor Olivier of the Policlinique diagnosed a menace of tuberculosis and prescribed as urgent a stay in the mountains. It was a great trial for Louisa, but she resigned herself to it.

In October, she left for Leysin where she was hospitalized in a chalet of Dr. Olivier's: "Hope," situated at LeFeydey, above Leysin at 4,200 feet altitude. From there, one could look out over the deep valley which descended to the Rhone River, opposite a panorama of mountains reaching from Les Diablerets to Les Dents du Midi.

The chalet was run by deaconesses. In front of the bedrooms stretched a wide gallery where the patients could take their cure by relaxing on a chaise-lounge in the radiant mountain sun. It was, at that time, the best—nay, the only—hope of curing or halting that dreaded illness, tuberculosis. The duration of the mountain cures varied according to the gravity of the cases. Certain sick people stayed only a month, while others never came back down from Leysin.

The doctor had prescribed for Louisa a stay of three months. But as her state of health did not improve, she remained there seven months, until the end of May, 1919. She was terribly bored during this long period of inactivity. Her letters, however, scarcely show it. One finds her always preoccupied with the cares of others.

Leysin was for Louisa, however, a privileged time of contact with other girls. Most of them came from very simple surroundings: salesgirls, housemaids or factory workers. They had more experience than she with the struggles of life. Others, like her, had gone to school or were still students. But almost all had other preoccupations than Louisa. She was very astonished by this fact but tried to understand them, without, however, approving of them. Affable with each, she made friends with only two or three in whom she perceived aspirations similar to her own. This would be the first of some beautiful friendships, notably her meeting Bluette de Blaireville, who was to become her confidante and most intimate friend.

Let us allow her to tell her impressions of her surroundings and the conclusions she drew for her own life. Between November 10th and 13th, 1918, she wrote to her brother, Alexander, a young substitute minister in a parish of the Canton of Vaud: ". . . I have near me a girl from La Chaux-de-Fonds whom I like very much; she is advanced and lends me all her books. Thank you for the reading that you sent me."

On the 13th: "I had to interrupt my letter; we had an eventful day. It was Monday, at the announcement of the Armistice. Naturally everything was decorated; joy, or rather a wild and general uproar overcame them all. They set aside their treatments on the chaise-lounges, left the ordinary discipline, to rejoice at their ease. There were corteges, noise, all night. It was still more sad than happy. My friend and I profited from this confusion to take a beautiful walk to a village below Leysin. In the evening there was still more animation. They allowed us to take a short walk, which calmed our spirits. We can imagine what it was like in the city.

"I think of you a lot, my dear Alexander. Are there still cases of the flu? I am happy to know that you are content with your job, which you like. I would like for you to come and preach here once. The minister is quite old and ought to stay with old people. Meanwhile the girls here need to be shaken in order to learn to be sincere and to take life seriously. . ."

A few days later, she corresponded with her sister Alice: "Yesterday evening, we had a party in honor of the sick who are going to leave. . .Bluette and I prepared a 'grab-bag' with an object for everyone, made with ingenuity! Bluette is without equal. The more I know her, the more I love her. In her personal life, she has had to suffer because there is so much greatness next to pettiness and ugly things that I can guess at. She is the oldest child in her family, and, although I am a month older than she, it seems to me that she is much older than I in many ways; she has lived in a way which is greatly different and profitable from the way I have lived. For example, she knows what it is to worry about one's daily bread, she has had a 'social life,' she keeps an impression of bitterness; one senses that she knows the burdens of life.

"I assure you that here I am learning to understand others better, and their needs. How many times have I brutally, though involuntarily, made them feel the difference in our education! All these girls earn their living. . .they are in the midst of everyday life, they undergo it docilely and reserve their strength for their private life, their families, their stories of drafted soldiers. I, who don't have these preoccupations, I hurt them so easily by my life apart. That is to tell you how much Bluette is superior to me because she knows better than I the difficulties of life. . . And then Bluette is courageous, more so than I who am Christian, she who is not. That is not to say that she is without fault, but I admire her and she makes me feel good."

Bluette spent only two months at Leysin. Louisa remained in touch with her through correspondence, and the friendship which blossomed there proved life-long. They helped each other find the sense of life. Later, it was Louisa who showed the way to Bluette, who followed soon after Louisa's conversion.

Through Bluette, also, Louisa made the acquaintance of Adrienne von Speyr, like her a soul thirsting for the absolute, a keen intelligence always in search of truth. Bluette had been Adrienne's classmate at the junior college of La Chaux-de-Fonds. They met again at Leysin in the same struggle against illness. A year younger than Louisa and Bluette, Adrienne surpassed them in the extent of her education and the depths of her reflections. Bluette invited her to come each week to the chalet "Hope" to give a lecture. "We are all falling asleep, we need some life." The project came to pass all the more easily because Adrienne was the cousin of the "Doctoress" Olivier, foundress of the chalet "Hope."

There is no reference to these conversations in Louisa's correspondence. However, Adrienne kept a precise memory of a conversation with her: ". . .these lectures were very particular hours, unforgettable guideposts in my existence. My themes were rather disconcerting! 'The Right to Think,' 'Obedience and Liberty,' 'Truth and Its Measure,' 'The Expression of Truth in the Works of Dostoevsky.' The audience were factory workers, young nurses and a few stu-

dents. One of them was Louisa Jaques. She was
around 20 years old [in fact, 18]. She had big, black
eyes, a slender build, slender white hands, a slightly
muffled voice. She accompanied me to the house
after the second or third lecture; there, as I was supposed to lie down, she remained near me.

" 'You will force me to become a Catholic,' said
Louisa at the moment of her departure.

" 'What do you mean?'

" 'Obedience and liberty meet in unity—as you
present it—only in God and in His Church.' . . . Later
Louisa dared to try the adventure; she became a
Catholic." (Adrienne von Speyr was received into the
Church in 1940.)

Louisa left Leysin on May 31, 1919. Nice weather
was setting in and her health seemed well re-
established. Right away she took up her old job with
the Horbers. The whole summer was spent preparing the definitive foundation of the "League for Post-
War Reforms." At the beginning of December, there
was a general assembly at Neuchatel. It was a question of deciding whether the League would continue
or not, since up to that point the members were
scarcely numerous.

Louisa, for her part, did not doubt the good that
this organization would accomplish; but it was necessary to overcome the resistance of her relatives. For
the first time after the war years, her father would
be able to return to Switzerland for a vacation.
Meanwhile, he had remarried and the family was
larger by two boys: Auguste and Eddy. They all were
to meet at L'Auberson for the holidays at the end
of the year. Louisa would have to justify her work-

ing for the League. Her family viewed this work with
a distrustful eye; it had a political side which did
not please them. Besides, that position did not offer
any future for their daughter. They wanted her to
give it up.

In mid-December, Louisa opened her heart to her
sister Alice: "In short, I don't fear the arguments
at Christmas; for me it is a question of mission and
conviction if I get involved in politics, it is not because I am looking for what pleases me the most.
Thus I am calm, feeling 'free' because, in harmony
with my conscience, I do not fear having to explain
myself. It is my ideal to be 'free': to have the strength
to do what I feel *I ought* to do, and I do not think
that that should afflict Papa or Mama."

We do not know anything about this meeting, but
Louisa did not succeed in convincing her father and
stepmother. Very much against her wishes, she left
Mr. Horber. In the month of May, 1920, when her
parents had left again for Africa, we find her working as an accountant for a lawyer in Lausanne, a
friend of her father's. She felt keenly her abandon-
ing the League. She felt a sacrifice of her liberty
which she put above everything. This sacrifice was
doubled by another; her parents took with them the
two oldest children: Alexander, who had finished his
studies for the ministry, and Elizabeth, who was a
nurse and had promised to serve the mission in this
capacity for six years. "Little Mother" now remained
at L'Auberson in the old family house. Louisa's sister Alice was a teacher in a girls' school and was
preparing to leave for America as soon as possible.

Louisa was desperately lonely in Lausanne. At the
time when she needed the affection of her family

the most, all of them went off in their own direction. For her, it was the monotonous life of a modest office worker. Worldly she never was—and frivolous, even less. Nature and music were her only hobbies. She did not miss a single outstanding spectacle or any of the major concerts of this time: the Pitoëffs, Cortot and Thibaud helped her put up with the pettiness of life.

In her work, she labored conscientiously and for a while devoted part of her nights to bringing up to date accounts that were ten years behind the times. This extra load was harmful to her health, but she did not let any of her troubles show. To read her letters to her family, one would believe she was the happiest of girls. Only the correspondence with her friends betrayed, here and there, the disappointments which assailed her.

Just the opposite of the Horbers, Louisa's new boss showed little philanthropy. He lacked even humanity and simple social justice in regard to his employees. It was not long before Louisa experienced that. Her salary was clearly insufficient; but she especially could not view with indifference the exploitation of which some other employees were victims. She did not utter a word to her parents, but she did not fail to show her indignation to her sister Alice. The latter could only encourage her to be patient. In an answer to Alice, Louisa examined her sentiments: "In short, I don't have any bitterness toward Mr. Y., nor against anyone. Sometimes I understand him. There are moments when I admire everyone. Life is a strange thing. One judges, one looks, but one does not see. The one who would know everything would pardon everything." She

ended with this advice: "Take care of your heart
more than anything else; everything which touches
on love is saved from death."

Louisa compensated for the avarice of her boss
through her own generosity. Her sister Alice relates
on this subject: "When Louisa was at Lausanne, she
went to visit sick people in poor slum dwellings. She
obtained the addresses through a society or through
acquaintances. What misery she discovered. When
I came to visit her, often she still had errands to
run; there were mysterious packages to place here
and there; but she never would let me enter with
her. She would say to me: 'The poor woman is dying;
for you to enter would be to expose yourself to tuberculosis. I have resisted it, I am cured of it.'

"Seeing her devote herself thus to others, I care-
lessly sent her all the extra money I earned; I did
not keep accounts. What was my surprise much
later—I think it was when I got married—when she
told me that she had invested in my name every
'centime' that I had given her, that it earned 8 per-
cent interest per year, and it was there waiting for
me." Spending everything she earned, she did not
concern herself with economizing or especially with
getting rich!

Finally, the behavior of her employer shocked her
too much. She left him in November 1921, and went
to see "Little Mother" at L'Auberson. Her work at
the lawyer's office in Lausanne had been a bitter dis-
appointment. Louisa had had the chance to put into
practice there what she confided to her sister about
an exiled Russian family: "Material difficulties give
great value to a life, but they complicate it also.
How much money can embellish life, not the money,

but the independence which it permits. Happy also are those who can be independent by their interior richness."

Up till then she had safeguarded this precious good in the middle of vexations. It would be harder to keep it in the course of trials which were to accumulate in her path in the following years. Already they seemed to provoke in her a religious crisis. For a while during this period, she stopped going to church. She showed herself to be critical or indifferent toward the religion of her childhood.

For the moment, she had rejoined "Little Mother," but the roles were reversed. It was Louisa who watched over the very weakened health of Aunt Alice. The latter never got over a bad case of the flu and had to stay in bed all of the time. Louisa was quite happy to fulfill this labor of gratitude. Then she used her free hours to get back to her studies. Would she perhaps manage to accomplish her goal of obtaining a B.A.? As soon as she arrived, she found a Latin teacher and began her lessons with enthusiasm.

L'Auberson was also a familiar environment with cousins and friends...and Louisa needed to be busy and surrounded by others, since at the beginning of December, her sister Alice left for America. She would remain there more than a year. The separation was sad. Certainly, Louisa loved her whole family profoundly. She was even offered a chance to go to see her parents and older brother and sister in the Transvaal. Several times they pressed her to go there. But Africa did not attract her, and besides, how could she abandon "Little Mother" who was sick? But especially her heart was more with her

sister Alice. She hoped she would come back soon.
If she stayed..."I will go to America," she declared
to a friend, "and I will search out a job of some
sort for myself. I cannot separate myself from Alice.
She is the best thing I have on this mean earth."

This friend came to visit her at L'Auberson. A few
days later, Louisa thanked her for her visit, which
had comforted her. At the end of Louisa's letter, there
is an expression of bitterness: "But tell me why there
is always a base of revolt in me and why I feel close
to the damned who live in Hell, this suffering of
those who cannot love? Under whatever aspect it
presents itself, life revolts me a little." She related
the sad adventure of a cousin gravely ill with nerves
and concluded: "Do you see, what makes me angry
is that life makes all of us criminals of all sorts
and irresponsible people."

She had a very clear sense of the unavoidable
necessity of sacrifice, a "religious" need of expiation, although her faith did not bring her any light
on this point. In a letter to her sister Alice, speaking of the affection which united her to her family,
she wrote: "I feel ever more clearly that what I have
that is sweet, loving, peaceful, I owe to you and to
Zab [Elizabeth]...One lives by the heart; it is from
the heart that flows all the richness and, for it to
be able to be generous, it must be possessed."

Her heart was fully taken over by the love of her
kin. "As a religion, I had only the cult of a daughter, the love of my kin," she would say in the story
of her conversion. "I needed their happiness." Therefore, she found it natural to be sacrificed or to sacrifice herself for them. And while she herself struggled
against discouragement, she sent to her sister Alice

messages like this: "Have courage, my dear, don't despair and don't get discouraged. There are not dark hours, as deep as they might be, which do not also bring riches." Speaking of Louisa's correspondence, her sister Alice would say, "I possess all the letters she wrote me—or almost—since 1918. They are all written to bring joy; they possess a contagious enthusiasm. She never lets her own preoccupations show...a great courage and immense faith in the future characterize her."

It is indeed with these dispositions that Louisa went up to L'Auberson. The more peaceful country life, the family surroundings, the visits for "Little Mother" and for herself certainly were a precious comfort for her. But the upkeep of the house and household, taking care of Aunt Alice, who most of the time got up only for a short while at the end of the day, absorbed her time and strength. "Little Mother" had always been authoritarian; sick and old, she became even more demanding. She wanted Louisa to be beside her constantly. The latter's cousins, who lived in the same house, testified that Louisa's patience in these circumstances was truly admirable. "It was really the life of a slave," wrote one of them, "but she fulfilled it with so much devotion."

In the month of April, 1922, with her professor absent, she had to give up her studies: "My project of getting a B.A.," she wrote, "fell in the water like a jewel I did not need to go after."

Toward autumn, "Little Mother's" health was far from getting better. With great regret, Louisa had to make the decision to return to Lausanne. Winter in the Jura was really too rough for Aunt Alice and for herself. They went and settled in the *pension* of Bethanie, kept by some deaconesses at Vallombreuse.

In the spring of 1923, they went back to the village, but material worries came and complicated the situation. The expenses which were caused by moving and the upkeep of the house were not covered by any income. They finally had to resolve, after many hesitations, to abandon the old home at L'Auberson once and for all. Starting the following autumn, Aunt Alice would remain hospitalized at Bethanie, and Louisa would again be in search of a job so she could earn her living.

After many fruitless attempts, she found work finally as a typist at Morges with a childhood friend, Miss Lydia von Auw, who was pursuing her theological studies at the Protestant faculty of Lausanne. She arrived there March 1, 1924. The next morning, Louisa slept until noon. Her friend, far from worrying, rejoiced, thinking this rest would do her good. The following day, Louisa called her from her window and showed her on the night table a basin full of blood which she had just spit up. The doctor, who was called immediately, prescribed rest and cold food.

Louisa got better and spent several days convalescing at the home of this family that loved her dearly and did their utmost to take good care of her. Louisa kept up her courage and her gaiety. The family doctor enjoyed chatting with her during his visits and teasing her when she spread out a deck of cards on the eiderdown to tell him the future. They were able to reach her parents through the intermediary of the Swiss Mission. It was decided at that time that Louisa would enter Bethanie, too, in order to take a treatment for tuberculosis. She arrived there March 20. The treatment was to last about two years.

There she was reduced to inactivity again, dependent on others for everything, with a very controlled diet. She resigned herself to it with difficulty. What did the future hold for her? On March 23, she wrote to her sister Alice, who was about to return from America: "Does anything exist that is more beautiful than the liberty of our acts and independence? To owe nothing to anyone, yes, it is beautiful...But perhaps love knows another degree where to receive and to give become similar things.

"I have earned nothing, but I have given what I was able to; in becoming poor, it is perhaps toward another richness that I am going."

Scarcely on her feet, but with the permission of her doctor, Louisa hunted for a job which would pay enough to meet the expenses of living in a *pension*. "I have a little occupation here which is very agreeable," she wrote to her friend, Bluette. "In the morning I read to a nice old man in the *pension* and I write his letters for him. Thus, I earn half my rent, and I am so happy with that transitory money."

A little later, she found something to take up the rest of her day. "I take nice walks with a little English girl whom I care for three afternoons a week. I am delighted to have another little job which permits me to earn my rent now."

These two extracts date from the end of her stay at Bethanie, in the spring of 1926. A peaceful mood reigns in them. Louisa, however, had just touched

the bottom of the abyss. To the forced inactivity of
these two years of treatment was added a moral trial,
or rather a temptation, which almost dragged her
into an adventure from which there was no exit.
In any case, it was the shipwreck of her religious
practice.

This trial had begun in the last months of her
stay at L'Auberson. The future was dim; no happy
prospect appeared before her. First it was the
worry—excessive, no doubt—about the happiness of
her family. Her older brother and sisters had left;
each one had found his own path in life, but she
thought about them constantly. She needed for them
to be happy, and as events frequently thwarted the
projects she conceived for them, she went from disillusionment to disillusionment. Nevertheless, she did
not forget her own future.

By this time, she was a good deal past her 20th
birthday; she, too, dreamt of marriage. But when?
To whom? The realization of this desire seemed to
be distant. Was she not tied down by her role as
nurse for "Little Mother"? Her correspondence
scarcely reveals this worry. Others, particularly Aunt
Alice, worried about it for her. At L'Auberson there
were one or two marriage proposals. Louisa refused.
"They ask me to marry them," she replied to her
aunt, "because I am the daughter of a minister."
In these suitors she did not find her ideal of love,
such as she described in one of her letters from Leysin: "There are some delicious temperaments here,
but there isn't a single one of them who knows what
love is. Love as I know it in my thoughts is stronger
than evil, more contagious than egoism, love which
creates."

It is possible that, if she had been a Catholic, Louisa might have been inclined to hear the call of the greatest love, the gift of oneself in a consecrated life. But the convictions of those around her fortified her against this attraction. Even the life of the Protestant deaconesses, whom she knew and revered, did not seem ever to have exercised an attraction for her. Perhaps she did not see in it the concrete realization of a life of love as she hoped for. Therefore, there was nothing left but settling in the world.

Now Louisa, whose moral life was so strict and whose demands of love were so high, nevertheless experienced the weaknesses of the human heart. She let herself be drawn into "going steady," and it was a guilty association. The doctor who took care of her aunt and, therefore, frequently came to the house, had understood Louisa's qualities of heart and greatness of soul. He appreciated her gaiety and courage. He felt more than esteem for her.

He began to court her. In the evening, after he had finished his rounds, he would invite her for a ride in his car. Aunt Alice was alarmed by these attentions. She sensed the danger right away. "This girl will drive me crazy!" she exclaimed in a dramatic tone in front of the cousins. She tried to oppose these dates with all her power. Louisa, who had resisted so easily and with such obstinacy other advances, let herself be captivated. More than sensitiveness, was it not kindness in the face of weakness that blinded her? The thought that she could console someone who was suffering? The doctor was not happy in his marriage.

The dates continued after her return to Lausanne.

Then Louisa had her relapse and entered the hospital at Bethanie. The doctor hurried to her bedside to encourage her, to assure her that she would recover her health. Soon his visits became regular. But as Louisa regained her strength, she realized the true nature of their sentiments. Her conscience showed her the irregularity and the dangers of this situation. At the beginning of December, 1924, she courageously made the decision to break off. She so informed the doctor and begged him never to come again. He respected her wishes, and she never saw him again.

In the following month of February, she learned that he was gravely ill. A few days later, on February 13, there came the painful news of his death.

The death of this young doctor, who left behind him a wife and two small children, caused much gossip in the region. Louisa heard in her surroundings that he had thrown prudence to the winds and had sought death. That report was probably exaggerated, but she was crushed by it. She felt directly responsible.

Without wanting to let anything show, she went to the funeral, discreetly taking a place in the last pew of the church. In her heart something was broken. For several weeks she kept quiet. It was only a month later that she gave free reign to her grief and remorse in the most desolate of her letters to Bluette, her intimate friend: ". . . What did I do to kill him? What did I do to kill the man I love? I did not know, I never thought I could drive him to despair. His love gave me life—why was mine so harmful? And yet I would have given him everything. It is because I believed that he would be happy for me to live that I preferred life to death. How mistaken I was! It would have been better for me just to die. You who understand, my Bluette, tell me why I killed the one I love. I know it is my fault, but I don't understand. . ."

She reproached herself for not having gone to visit him when she heard he was hospitalized. "Thus we were separated without leaving each other, or rather we left each other the way we met, suddenly, without knowing why. It seemed to me that I had always known him, always loved him, as if love had no beginning; I wish it didn't have any end, either. . ." Bluette was the only person to whom she confided her distress. But even in this letter of April 17, 1925, Louisa regained her self-control to ask for news, to be interested in others. She ended the letter: "I don't have the courage to re-read this awful letter. Excuse me for having written you this way. I will not begin my complaints again."

The months passed without bringing any great changes in her life. Her sister Alice had returned from America in October, 1924. She was taking courses at Geneva with the goal of obtaining a degree in library science. She often came to spend a few days with Louisa and her aunt. She had become engaged in the United States and was preparing to go back to see her fiance during the upcoming summer vacation. She wanted Louisa to rejoin their family in Africa before winter. Louisa was scarcely enthusiastic for this departure. In her heart, she dreamt of finding something which would permit her to stay near her sister Alice.

The tuberculosis treatment was nearing its end. The menace of the illness seemed to be turned aside; the last X-rays showed clear lungs.

Louisa was able to go to a few concerts and even to get away a few days for meetings organized at Thonon under the auspices of the International League of Women for Peace and Liberty. There she met Bluette again and through her made the acquaintance of Miss Verena Pfenninger, a friend who would play a decisive role in her conversion.

The impulsive chatter of her correspondence this year, 1925, hides the interior drama: "All those whom I love profoundly have been taken away from me," she wrote to Bluette. Alice's marriage was now only a matter of months. Her sister was going to leave her definitively. "Little Mother" was still weaker and more difficult to satisfy. The death of the doctor remained like a wound in Louisa's heart. Her own material future never stopped causing her worry either. Cured, she would have to hunt for a job and lodgings, and both were not easy to find at this time. She felt so alone.

Did God see her solitude? But who is God? Did He know the suffering of His children?

This string of setbacks, or relapses in her health, broke her drive. She had long since abandoned religious practice; a quiet revolt which discouraged all prayer entered her.

In her confusion, she saw only one source of help, her friend Bluette. She wanted to go to La Chaux-de-Fonds to see her and chat with her. She needed the warmth of her friendship. On January 17, 1926, she wrote to her: "I have a great desire to see you, Bluette. Would it bother you if I visited you for two days? I hesitate, I scarcely dare ask it because I am afraid it will bother your mother and you, but I have such a strong desire to see you."

The answer arrived without delay. Bluette would be overjoyed to welcome her. The meeting was set for the 13th and 14th of February.

2

CONVERSION AND VOCATION
(1926 - 1938)

Louisa's visit to Bluette changed the whole direction of her life. She had reached the conclusion that God did not exist—life had no meaning. It was in this state of despair that she retired on the night of February 13, 1926. "Oh, to die, to die. . ." Lying on her bed utterly crushed by the events of the past few years, she suddenly saw a woman dressed as a nun enter through the window. The woman was tall and straight and seemed to be out of breath, as if she had been running. She stood close to the bed, and Louisa sensed this was a real person. She could see her breathe and turn her head. Frightened, Louisa turned away and closed her eyes. When she opened them later, the woman was still there and remained for a good part of the night. Nothing was said, but hope stirred in Louisa's heart. As a result of this vision, Louisa resolved that before giving up all hope in God, she would enter a convent and pray. Looking back, she called this experience "the exclusive cause of an irresistible attraction toward the cloister."

All that we know of Louisa, her sense of balance, her critical sense, and her cult of truth guarantees the sincerity of this account and bears witness in favor of the authenticity of the reported incident. The

sobriety of her own account of this apparition proves
Louisa's intention of saying only what she was sure
of, without adding personal interpretations. Apart
from a guarded reference in the morning to her
friend that during the night she "had seen a statue
at the foot of my bed—a nun," she would for years
keep secret this event which turned her life around.

This apparition was not a dream; Louisa insisted
on that point. It came while she was awake. Could
it have been a product of the subconscious? What
could one say in support of this supposition? This
person in the night did not answer a prayer. She
broke into Louisa's life and contradicted the very
basis of her thought. Moreover, Louisa was unable
to identify her and did not try to do so. She saw
something like a "nun" in a dress which she did
not know, but later thought she recognized as the
habit of the Poor Clares.

There was no message. The apparition did not
speak. It was a presence. After the fright of the first
instant, Louisa had a presentiment of a beneficial
protectress who hastened toward her to watch over
her. The final impression was not a troubled mind
but peace and a firm resolution.

The decisive element, which should make us admit
the reality of this incident, was its consequences.
In an instant, Louisa's life was changed by it. From
despair, from obscurity on existence and love of God,
she passed to certitude, which, let us note, went
against everything she had believed up until then.
A religious, the convent...that is Catholicism! She
was not completely ignorant of that religion, but
her acquaintance with it was especially made of
prejudices. There was in her an innate repulsion,

inherited from her surroundings, against that "degenerate" Church.

More than anything for her whose love for her family was her only religion, this would be betraying her family. She would go that far. . . "but when my father dies; there is no use causing him that sorrow." Louisa, therefore, was quite right to see in this mysterious messenger's entrance, the point of departure for her conversion. It was the overturning of her whole life to seek and accomplish the will of God.

The morning after this event, Louisa returned to Bethanie. From that day on her letters were more peaceful. She felt courage again and she was waiting for something, but this wait was confident.

The tuberculin treatment finally ended, Louisa left Bethanie on April 20, 1926. She had spent two years and one month there.

The marriage of her sister Alice took place on July 16. A week later, the young couple left to live in America. Louisa's family asked her to come to Africa, but she wanted to remain in Switzerland near her aunt. In spite of all her efforts, Louisa still had not found a job there. Finally, on August 30, a favorable response arrived from Milan. She would begin her work on October 1. She confided to Alice: "I am sorry to leave 'Little Mother' but that's life—separation."

A passage in this letter tells us better than many words how she had taken interest in life since the encounter in February: "Last week there was a marvelous concert; violinist: Thibaud; pianist: Cortot. It was splendid. Thibaud plays divinely and Cortot is a fantastic virtuoso who makes you 'vibrate' for hours that seem both short and infinite like eternity. The audience was delirious. This music gave me the desire to play some music again. I bought for myself a notebook by Heller, the minuet by Paderewski. I've taken up again my notebooks of Grieg and Bach; the piano on the third floor of Isola Bella (a *pension* not far from Bethanie) welcomes me with good will."

The post Louisa obtained in Milan was as governess to a small boy. In the first news sent from there to Bluette, she recounted her departure: "The goodbyes to Aunt Alice came off without any painful scenes; (she) showed herself to be so sweet, so friendly that it was done as if it were nothing." Then she gave her first impressions of her little pupil. "He is a good little kid who does not have a bad nature, although he likes to act as terrible and mean as possible... In the beginning I was a little astonished to see flying toward the ceiling what was supposed to serve as his toilette and I can't keep from laughing remembering his piteous air when he learned that he was supposed to pick up everything himself and wipe up his inundations. He has the innate habits of a great overlord and quite sincerely he repeated: 'But you are here to wash my feet, and Therese comes in the morning to wipe up the water I spill.' I, who am a good little democrat, I have much more prosaic habits and I am teaching him that everyone must pick up what he drops. For the moment, it is the reign of justice which he finds sufficiently hard; later, perhaps, he will learn courtesy."

Louisa was free every day while the child was in school from 8 a.m. to 4 p.m. Much of this time was

spent in visiting churches. One day, in the church
of Santa Maria delle Grazie, she happened to be
present at Benediction of the Blessed Sacrament.
It was October, the month of the Rosary. Each evening there was recitation of the Rosary and Benediction of the Blessed Sacrament. Louisa's reaction was
one of complete incomprehension, although she felt
drawn to pray there. She never seemed to be able
to pray enough.

A year was spent in this way. During the winter,
Louisa read *Maggy,* the story of Margaret Lekeux,
written by her brother Father Martial Lekeux,
O.F.M. The book was sent to her by Bluette. In
thanking her, Louisa wrote: "I wept like a Magda-
len before such a beautiful life. You always send me
books that dazzle me." Although not at all drawn
to become a Catholic, she began attending daily
Mass. She did not understand, nor even care about
what was happening at the altar, but there was
something that irresistibly attracted her.

About this time, Louisa learned that her friend
Verena Pfenninger had become a Catholic. Verena
was at that time teaching in a school at Tirana,
in Albania. Louisa had met her at the meetings at
Thonon during the summer of 1925. She was as-
tounded at this conversion because she had always
equated Catholicism with superstition and ignorance, and Verna was a very intelligent and capable
person.

In the month of May, Bluette invited Louisa to
spend a few days later in the summer with her and
some friends, among them Verena. Louisa accepted
happily and joined the group on the 4th of August.
Verena sensed the turmoil in Louisa's heart and one

evening confided her wish that Louisa could share in the help the Lord Jesus gives: "He who is so great, makes Himself very small in order to come to us, hidden under the appearance of bread, so as to help us. . . if only you knew. . ." These words awakened in Louisa an intense desire to receive Jesus, with the confidence that then she would be healed. From this time on, there was something on the altar and in the Mass that she seemed to understand, although she still had no wish to become a Catholic. Was not this desire evidence of the silent attraction of grace? Later Our Lord was to speak of this period in Louisa's life: "You came to ask Me for help through My Sacraments. My grace resuscitated you."

From the time of summer vacation Louisa's longing to receive Communion did not lessen in intensity. She strongly felt the need to purify her heart in order to prepare herself for meeting the Lord. Before even approaching the confessional, she wanted to rectify the least failings in her life. It was thus that she declared to her friend Bluette on September 5: "I have decided never again to tell any lie and I am shaking myself free of all disagreeable memories: let the wind carry them off with the dead leaves! I remember having lied to you long ago in Geneva by saying that I was thinking of you when I was very occupied with thinking about myself! You had asked me what I was thinking about; it is stupid, but I have never forgotten that; do you see, I am getting rid of it by telling it to you. I believed I would never tell it to you because I was so ashamed of having thus flattered your affection. You will forgive me for it, won't you? I can't recall anything else, otherwise I would own up to it, since I will never tell another lie now."

Louisa also felt that she ought to go to confession. "The decision which I was about to make weighed very heavily upon me...I felt my whole life depended upon it." Louisa realized this might cause an irreparable break with her family. She also had all the horror of the confessional that centuries of Protestantism had bred. "But I wanted to do it." Finally, one day in November, she went to the cathedral, entered the confessional and informed the priest that she was a Protestant who wanted to go to confession in order to receive Jesus. The priest asked, "You want to receive Holy Communion? So you want to become a Catholic?" "No. I only want Holy Communion." After explaining that one cannot receive Holy Communion just like that—it is necessary to have religious instruction since it is a Sacrament—the priest gave her a note and sent her to the Sisters of the Cenacle.

It took Louisa ten days to overcome her fear of nuns and convents, and finally present herself at the convent door. There she met Madre Reggio, who won her heart at once. From then until March, 1928, Louisa met with the Madre for one or two hours each day except Sunday. It was a time of wonder and revelation for her! Problems that had bothered her from childhood seemed to unravel and straighten out. Not that everything was perfectly clear—the process of conversion takes time. Also, Madre Reggio's hearing was somewhat impaired, and Louisa's timidity kept her from pressing questions. This would cause difficulty later on, but for the time being, Louisa felt, "I had met my God."

At the end of January, 1928, Louisa's visa had not

been renewed because she did not have a work permit. She had to return again to Switzerland for several days while the lady she worked for multiplied efforts to keep her. This short stay permitted Louisa to visit "Little Mother" again, whom she rejoiced to find much better. Louisa returned to Milan to prepare for her Baptism, which had been set for March 18.

It was but a brief respite; on March 12 at 5:30 in the morning, Aunt Alice entered her eternity. Warned in time, Louisa hurried back to Switzerland, arriving soon enough to assist "Little Mother" in her last moments. After taking care of the burial and disposing of the little property that was left, Louisa returned to Milan.

Much work was waiting for her because her patrons also returned from several days' absence. Just the same, she obtained permission "to eclipse myself for three days of retreat (at the Cenacle), which had already been planned for a long time, and my Baptism took place quite peacefully. Here I am quite happy," she wrote to Bluette: "a new life!"

It was Sunday, March 18. A last minute change of time had resulted in Mme. Sophia Ferrario replacing the chosen godmother. This arrangement proved providential, as Mme. Sophia Ferrario understood Louisa and her attraction to the religious life. "I believe it is due to the help which I found in her, together with Madre's vigilance, that I was able to respond to my vocation."

The next day, the Feast of St. Joseph, Louisa made her First Communion. She enjoyed no sensible consolations or experiences, but she had not expected any. For her it was enough that Jesus had come into her life.

While Communion was a source of great joy to her, confession remained a source of trial and consternation. When preparing for her Confirmation a few weeks after her Baptism, Louisa returned to the confessional to correct a previous confession in which she felt she had not told the whole truth. It was for her the occasion of a painful act of humility. She confided the incident to Father Sylvére, her confessor in Jerusalem. At her preceding confession, the confessor had asked a question concerning a circumstance exterior to the fault confessed, a circumstance which changed neither the culpability nor the nature of the failing. Surprised by this unexpected questioning, her answer had been materially false. Upset, she did not dare speak up to rectify it. But anxiety invaded her soul. Before receiving Confirmation, she wanted to free herself from it and she returned to the confessional to correct it. This act of humility was recompensed by a permanent grace. Louisa hurried away to another church to receive Holy Communion. "I can still see the spot where I knelt near a column after having received Our Lord: ah, it was as though I had swallowed some of the sun!... I have only experienced such a Communion that one unforgettable time. Later when doubts attacked me, when I no longer knew where I was or what I was doing, I clung to the Eucharist *because of that Communion.*"

In the month of May, her family still did not know of her conversion, but they sensed some event was in the offing and were worried about her because of her isolation. When they learned of her entrance into the Church, they were dismayed, but the grief

which they felt only accentuated their feelings of
affection toward the prodigal child. They felt they
were a little responsible, thinking they had not been
close enough to her. They wanted to prove that she
remained their beloved child and that the door was
always open to her.

On her side, Louisa had only one desire: to lead
her family to the same light. "The happiness that
one finds in the Church, I cannot utter it. I would
love for all my family to know it and better than
I, all those who are dear to me," she confided to
Bluette. To love her family, that meant to her to
become a sign which showed them the way. She
wanted to reveal to them the tenderness, but also
the demands of God's love. This conversion would
sometimes lead her to mark with harshness the
necessary break.

On both sides there was much suffering, a fruitful
suffering certainly, even if it did not end in uniting
the family in the same faith while Sister Mary of
the Trinity was still alive. By her life which was
totally given to the Lord, Louisa was a question
mark for her family and friends. God alone, who
reads the depth of hearts, knows the answers which
were given.

Bluette came to Milan in June for her vacation,
which was spent at the Cenacle where she made
a ten-day retreat in preparation for her Baptism.
She was the first to follow Louisa into the Church;
other friends would follow. Her Baptism and First
Communion took place on the Feast of St. John the
Baptist, with Confirmation following shortly thereafter. While at the Cenacle, Bluette spoke to Madre
Reggio of Louisa's desire for religious life, something

Bluette had sensed. Madre Reggio feared that
Louisa's health was too poor, but later urged Louisa
to make inquiries as to the possibility of entering
a convent.

Having returned together to Switzerland during
their vacation, Louisa and Bluette visited the Visitation Nuns of Fribourg on Sunday, July 22. In spite
of the scant attraction which she felt during this
first meeting with the cloistered life, Louisa left with
the certainty that she would enter the convent, but
where? An inner voice seemed to say: "When you
have found your place in the Church, they will all
come to seek you, and thus you will make them consider the Church!" Before leaving Switzerland,
Louisa disposed of the remaining household belongings of Aunt Alice, keeping only what was strictly
necessary.

Shortly after Louisa's return to Milan, the family
for whom she worked had to dismiss her because
of financial reversals. Just at this point her father
wrote asking her to come to Africa, promising to
pay for her return to Milan at the end of two years
if she was not happy with them. They also offered
her a trip to America to visit Alice, whom she loved
so much.

Louisa chose to remain in Milan where a friend,
governess in the household of Countess Borromeo,
helped her obtain a position with the Countess
Agliardi, sister to Countess Borromeo. There were
three children, and Louisa was to care for the oldest, a boy, aged three and a half years. As the Countess Agliardi wanted the children raised according
to the Montessori method, Louisa first entered (on
October 4) the home of Countess Borromeo to serve

an apprenticeship in this method. Three days later she suffered a severe hemorrhage.

A doctor she consulted assured her that although the disease was advanced, there were no Koch bacilli present; therefore, there was no danger of contagion. It was the consistent absence of the bacilli that made it morally possible for Louisa to offer herself to religious life and to the care of children. She kept silent about this attack, and managed to complete the training.

The Countess Agliardi was staying at her country estate near Bergamo, and Louisa joined the family there. The fresh air and sunlight were exactly what she needed. It seemed that her health problem was taking care of itself. And then, one evening about a month after her arrival at the estate, Louisa suddenly felt that she was dying. She was able to get to her room without anyone noticing. Her greatest anxiety was not concerned with death, or with leaving her family, but "I have not had time to become a nun." She prayed as never before, promising God that if He let her live she would do something about her vocation without delay. The clots of blood she coughed up later in the evening and during the night convinced her that the hemorrhage had taken place internally.

Louisa had found in the Countess Agliardi more a friend than a mistress, and she was very happy with this family. A coincidence brought them even closer together: "Imagine," Louisa wrote to Bluette, "that the Countess told me the other evening that she goes to confession in Milan, since she found there an admirable confessor after some searching. And then we discovered that we have the same confessor!" Very devout, the Countess understood Louisa's desire and tried to help her find a religious community that would accept her. After many interviews and visits to various religious houses, Louisa was finally accepted by the Little Sisters of the Assumption in Milan. Final approval had to be obtained from the Superiors at the Motherhouse in Paris. Louisa had to go there for a ten-day retreat. At the same time, Alice wrote begging her to come to America. She was ill and expecting her second baby. Louisa went to Paris. Once again forgetful, she set out without her passport. Countess Agliardi accomplished a real race against the clock to get it to her at the last minute in the train station in Milan. Louisa arrived in Paris with a "very small suitcase and the inseparable photographs of my sisters whom I loved so much...a sore throat...also a temperature, quite a fever." The community was kind, but did not accept her.

Her interior disquiet, her attachment to her family unfavorably impressed the Mistress of Novices. Louisa was mistaken, perhaps, on the meaning of this anguish, which would be renewed several times in her attempts at religious life. She attributed her anguish to her weakness, to her lack of generosity... Was it not an indication that God wanted her elsewhere? May we also see in these trials the gentle work of grace? "And immediately, one right after the other, I asked great sacrifices of you. Then you began to love Me. You loved Me ardently, wanting to give Me all your strength, all your time, all the affection in your heart, every breath of your life...And you emptied yourself out, you emptied yourself out..."

She related to Bluette: "The Little Sisters in Paris are charming; what energy and what wit! I had the impression of touching perfection with my fingers; the whole institution is admirably organized, and then they are so intelligent, these French women, they are very observant. They declared that their order was not for me. . . I was stunned! Don Giorgio [her confessor in Milan] thinks that since I found the door closed to me there, it is perhaps a sign that I should go to Alice. . ."

The return to Milan was sad. Louisa was still very sick with a temperature of 104°, and the Countess had hired another governess. Louisa went to see Madre Reggio and in her agitation rejected the Madre's advice. "She was right. But her decision caused an indescribable revolt in me—with the devil's help." So disturbed was Louisa by the seeming intransigence of Madre Reggio that she left her brusquely, indignant. Upon leaving the Cenacle, Louisa took the tramway to return home, full of resentment. But when she got off the tram, she saw the flower sellers on the square. She bought the most beautiful bouquet of white roses she could find and, retracing her steps, took it to Madre Reggio. The next morning at Communion, she heard this interior message: "Together we will achieve something. You can achieve nothing by yourself."

Louisa found another position in Milan. The work was easy. "The little girl whom I am to take care of is bigger than I am. She will be 18 in a few days, and she is very nice; she gives me no worries and no trouble; there never was a nicer job for me," she wrote to Bluette. As the young lady slept late each day, Louisa was able to attend an early Mass and visit one or two convents each morning. "I had made a list of all the convents that were suggested to me— it was a long page full—and I told Our Lord that I would take it as a sign of His will that I go to my sister if I reached the end of the list without being accepted."

When she had reached the last address on her list, Louisa was welcomed by the Franciscan Missionary Sisters of Egypt in Mesocco. The date of entrance was set at her first interview. Upon returning home, she found a cable from Alice telling her that a berth was reserved for her on a liner to America, and there was a check to cover all other expenses. In the same letter to Bluette of June 12, 1929, she announced to her, ". . .we have come to a delightful conclusion; listen to me carefully and help me to thank Jesus: October 15, I will enter as a postulant at the convent of the Franciscan Missionary Sisters of Egypt. It was arranged all by itself. I don't know why at the last minute when I was going to leave for America, since God did not send me any response other than a telegram from Alice. . . I answered Alice that I would go on condition that I be back before October 15, and I think that if she no longer agreed to send for me for so short a time, she would telegraph the next day. That is where we stand now."

To refuse this magnificent offer caused Louisa tremendous pain and suffering. To add to her trials, another letter soon arrived, this time from her father. He and Louisa's stepmother, and Alex and his wife were planning to come to Switzerland for a holiday the following May. Her parents planned to land in Genoa, meet Louisa and take her to Switzerland

with them. Against the advice of her doctor, Louisa
entered the convent instead, with the idea of offering her life for the conversion of her family. This
doctor, who knew well the convent and its dampness, had advised her to wait until spring since to
enter in the fall, to face winter with her precarious
health, would be to tempt God. Her reaction to that
was: "I will not last long, and so I will offer up my
life for the conversion of my family." Louisa's confessor said to her later: "People think it is easy to
die, but it is very difficult." One does not decide the
hour of one's death! Louisa still had a long way to
go to learn how to let herself be led by God.

Whether for herself or in regard to her family, one
must recognize that this decision was not prudent
from the human point of view, not even charitable;
nevertheless, it was love that pushed Louisa to act
thus: love of the Lord, to leave everything for Him,
and also love of her family, to obtain for them
through her sacrifice the grace of the true Faith.
Much later she was to write: "I would not do now
what I did then. Our Lord has made me understand
that to the supernatural means of sacrifice and
prayer we must add a great care not to neglect any
of the natural means which predispose souls to seek
and to welcome grace."

Her prayer and her offering certainly obtained
some lights for her family. Without approving of her
determination, they accepted from this moment on
to let her follow her own route. There was in their
attitude a profound respect and even a certain admiration.

On October 16, Louisa related her arrival in the
community of Mesocco: "Therefore I came yester-

day evening about seven p.m. It was already dark; my godmother Madame Ferrario accompanied me. They didn't expect me anymore; all the doors were closed, bolted. We waited a good while in the courtyard. It seemed they did not want me. Finally a window was opened, they muttered something incomprehensible in Milanese. Then we waited, rang again; the window opened twice more, then finally a light and some noise behind the door which opened. And one hears stories about kidnapping girls for the convent! In my case, I had rather to force the citadel to enter."

The winter was one of great suffering for Louisa. The dampness of the convent aggravated her illness, and the cold was a great trial. She suffered a severe hemorrhage several weeks after her entrance but concealed it, hoping to live long enough to become a novice. With the beginning of Advent, a psychological reaction set in. It took the form of a mad revolt and so affected Louisa that she begged to be sent away. Once she was calm, she realized how far removed this request was from her real intent.

However, she did not let any of this show in a letter to Countess Agliardi, dated December 15, the third week of Advent: "It has been two months since I have come here! It is a peaceful little convent, simple, simple. Here one lives in the shadows, in poverty and contentment. It seems to me that the good God made me fall into a little corner made especially for me: I am happy to be in a Franciscan house, they pray well here. My difficulties and my concern relate to my family. I am telling you this so that you might remember me a little in your prayers."

Years later, the Sister sacristan of Mesocco remembered Louisa. She spoke of her goodness and courage but added: "She was pitiful; she would have liked to undertake the material labor of the house with the others but could not, feeble and delicate as she was."

In April, Louisa was refused admittance to the community, and the "frightful inner pain" of inner revolt left her immediately, abruptly. "I would not have left on my own initiative—I would rather have died." The superiors kept her with them until the end of May so she could recover her health. When her family arrived, Alexander and his wife came to visit her at the convent, but her father could not bring himself to do this. Inexorable in her resolutions, Louisa had decided on her part that she would not leave the convent for this visit. It was on the advice of the Mother Provincial and the Countess Agliardi, alerted by the Superior, that Louisa consented to go to the hotel. The nun and the mother of a family each made her understand that she could not treat her family so severely. God certainly did not want her to impose on herself nor especially to impose on her father such a sacrifice. This moving meeting between father and daughter, the first in ten years, took place during the first days of May, 1930.

Upon leaving Mesocco, Louisa obtained a position as secretary and companion to the mother of Countess Agliardi. Don Giorgio advised Louisa to pursue her vocation, and the Franciscan Sisters of the Infant Jesus agreed to accept her if she were cured. With the little money she had on hand, Louisa went to Lourdes to beg for this cure. She says little of

this pilgrimage in her writings, but that little is
all the more eloquent because of its brevity: "Ah,
Lourdes!...I found the Blessed Virgin there...
Since then she has been a part of my life..." Before
leaving Lourdes, she felt she was cured, and a doctor who examined her on her return to Milan
declared there was absolutely nothing wrong with
her lungs. However, when the doctor for the Franciscan Sisters examined her, he declared that her
lungs were in a very bad state. Can the burst of
fervor of these days explain her apparent cure?

The evidence of her relapse renewed her uncertainty; at least it spared her a new attempt at religious life which did not correspond to her calling
and which might have consummated the ruining of
her health.

A letter arrived from her family in Switzerland,
asking her to come to them. As there was no reason
to refuse, Louisa joined them at L'Auberson. There
she really needed the defense of her father and
brother, since among the relations and acquaintances, all did not have the same broadness of mind
and the same comprehension for one whom they
regarded as a renegade.

Following the advice of her confessor, Louisa asked
her parents to pay for a series of tuberculin injections in the hope that these would cure her. Her
parents agreed, contingent on her promise not to
enter a convent. They feared that if she did so, the
illness would only return. When Louisa informed
them that the sole reason for taking the injections
was so that she could follow her vocation, they
yielded. She commented on this time together: "My

parents were very good to me. Papa consulted the specialist, paid for an expensive X-ray photograph and bought me some summer dresses and a winter coat, as I had given away nearly all my belongings. In spite of their kindness and the apparent peace that reigned amongst us (we carefully avoided any discussion on religion), we did not have ten minutes' happiness together. A chasm had opened up between us."

Before leaving for Africa on September 10, the Jaques family arranged for Louisa to live with her brother and his wife, who were to remain in Switzerland for the year. Mr. Jaques would send money for Louisa's support since her health was too poor for her to get a job. At the last minute, through her friend Bluette, a door opened for Louisa. Bluette wrote of a Catholic home in the mountains which took boarders at moderate rates. There Louisa could get rest, the good mountain air she needed, and have a Catholic church close by. The family agreed that she should go there.

When Louisa moved into the St. Agnes Home, she was surprised and delighted to find a chapel with the Blessed Sacrament in the house. This puzzled her since the Church was just across the road, but after several weeks she learned that the Home was run by The Society of the Daughters of the Heart of Mary. This religious congregation was founded during the French Revolution by Marie Adelaide de Cicé and the Jesuit Father Pierre de la Cloriviere. From the fact of its origin, a time of persecution, and in order to be able to work in all milieus, the members of the Society remain in lay clothes. They live alone or in small communities without letting it be known publicly that they belong to a religious society. The Novice Mistress was a good friend of Bluette, and a person whom Louisa greatly admired and loved. After Louisa had been in the Home for several months, the Novice Mistress asked her if she would like to join the Society. At the urging of Don Giorgio, she did so, becoming a postulant at Neuchâtel on February 22, 1931.

For Louisa, this stay appeared as a detour from the path to the cloister, but Don Giorgio judged correctly that this sojourn was providential. It is certain that the Society and particularly the Mistress of Novices of La Chaux-de-Fonds greatly influenced Louisa. As a recent convert, she still had much to learn about the Church. Her companion in the novitiate was also a convert. The congregation was particularly suited to the instruction of converts since it had been founded to work in the midst of Protestants. Louisa herself wrote at a later date: "I deeply loved the Society. Its mission in the world attracted me because it was one of my heart's greatest desires. Its very hidden and very deep union with the Blessed Virgin, which was the principle of all its actions, was an immense treasure. . . I owe a great deal to the Society. I have not regretted for one minute having entered that path." This stay, nevertheless, was only a stepping stone for her. Not until she had given all to the Lord in the cloister would Louisa experience peace in her soul.

On August 26, 1931, Louisa made her oblation, and began her teacher training at the Normal School. Her parents were overjoyed at her decision, since they could understand a vocation to teaching and working in the world to benefit others. Her father paid for her tuition and for the tuberculin treatments during her two years of training. These treatments resulted in a complete cure.

The school was a great trial for Louisa because of her natural reserve and timidity. She found herself the oldest student and the only Catholic in the class. One of the teachers made a profession of atheism and never missed an occasion to make fun of Christian beliefs. One day he assailed the divinity of Christ. Louisa asked for the floor: very calmly and with great gentleness she proved clearly through the Holy Scriptures the divinity of the Saviour. The fact was reported to the Protestant ministers of the city. The following Saturday, one could read in the bulletin of the Protestant parish an article deploring the lack of courage on the part of the students and concluding thus: "Honor to the young Catholic who was able to defend the divinity of Christ."

Louisa received her diploma from Normal School on April 3, 1933, and was sent to teach at Neuchâtel. That summer, her two sisters came to Switzerland. Elizabeth's husband had just died, and she was not well. She needed the comfort and consolation her sisters could give. Alice and her family came from America for their vacation. It was a happy reunion for the three sisters, the first in 13 years, but also the occasion for many secret sacrifices on Louisa's part since, as a member of the Society of the Daughters of the Heart of Mary, her time was not her own. Alice returned to America on September 1, but Elizabeth remained at Neuchâtel, where Louisa was teaching, until March, 1934.

Our principal source of information—Louisa's letters—is very poor for this period. Very busy with her work, she wrote little—besides which, there was little occasion to write; her sisters visited her, her best friends were nearby. Fortunately we have excellent testimony written by her companion in the novitiate of La Chaux-de-Fonds and at the school in Neuchâtel. Better than correspondence, these memories show us how she appeared to those around her: "I met Louisa for the first time at La Chaux-de-Fonds...Very tiny, she trotted around the silent little house as if hunting for a service to render. And when she looked at us, one had the impression of a look from beyond which penetrated into one's conscience. Affable, with a gentleness which I have never again found...attentive to her neighbor and eager to disappear in front of others, that's the way Louisa appeared to me when we first met."

At Neuchâtel later: "A deeper acquaintance with Louisa permitted me to discover her intelligence, an astonishing perspicacity in the psychological domain—her writing is proof—an intuitive intelligence, a general culture which she tried to hide through modesty, a very pronounced artistic sense— she felt and understood music; she wrote delightful poems rich in inspiration...she had wit but no mockery ever.

"Only in April, 1946, did I hear of the death of Sister Mary of the Trinity. Therefore it's not under the emotion of her death and her Notes that I spoke of her—invariably, during the years—in these simple terms: 'For me, Miss Jaques is the image of living saintliness.' And when someone asked me: 'What did she do?' I always gave this response: 'I never heard her pronounce a word against charity.'

"In spite of her feeble health, she wanted to practice some exterior penances. Not having received permission to do without butter at breakfast, she put the whole piece in her hot coffee and swallowed her drink without batting an eye, all at once; then she ate her bread dry.

"She was so thin she must have felt the cold more painfully than the other sisters. Never once did she complain, and yet her hands had dark spots, full of chilblains, and one saw her tremble...Her family had given her a fur coat; this coat was a nightmare for her. Her Superior wanted her to wear it when it was very cold in winter, but Louisa suffered very much because of it. Not lacking humor, she said, 'I am a pauper in a fur coat!'

"We all put her patience to the test...In the face of humiliations which were not spared her, she remained without bitterness, persuaded that the others were right...One remained disarmed in the presence of such self-effacement, such humility.

"When one saw her pray, one was seized with respect. Straight, motionless, her hands joined, scarcely leaning on the armrest, one felt that this soul was truly in conversation with or in admiration before God. I have never met anyone else who gave me, as she did, the feeling of being in the presence of a mystery to be respected."

At Neuchâtel, Louisa taught school. Her companion, also a teacher, continued: "Her great gentleness made difficult for her a task which is always for everyone not without problems. Louisa had great difficulty, it must be said, in maintaining discipline. She was not made for an active life, for guiding a troop of children who were more or less well brought up. Louisa was certainly successful in the families where she worked as a teacher but not in a school situation. The reason for that is very simple: she was like a fish out of water."

The curate of the parish also spoke of Louisa's difficulty in leading a class. Something in her kept her from imposing her will, from commanding. Her good will was evident, her principles excellent, but only for personal contacts or little groups.

From this period we have these resolutions of Louisa:

"Jesus! Education!

"1. To keep my word.
   When I go back on my word, to explain as far as possible why.
"2. To give an order, a counsel, an indication *once,* twice at the maximum.
"3. Soberness of words.
   Silence. Example, example, example.
"4. Not a *single* word (except in the necessity of getting information) which might lower others in the esteem of those who hear me. No flattery. But see beauty and make it be discovered. Not a *single* word which might be advantageous to me. To be quiet about myself. I don't exist anymore. There is only *Jesus* who is trying to reveal Himself through me.
"5. Never a reproach. Never recall the good done. It is given to God. In sanctions, the least words possible. Make the disapproval be felt.
   Make reparation, myself, if possible.
   Think about the Lord's judgments: 'Go and sin no more!'
"6. *Liberty* as much as possible so that generosity can grow and be practiced better. Demand by

example.
"7. Develop the sense of *independence,* and of in-
    dividual *responsibility.*
"8. Learn to keep *free* one's heart, one's will, to pos-
    sess oneself in order to *give* oneself and not to
    let oneself be taken in.
"9. Favor everything which nourishes personal life,
    desire for perfection, solitude with God."

When the time came for Louisa to take her vows,
the resignation of her Superior at Neuchâtel because
of ill health caused a delay which was to last six
months. Also, as Louisa had revealed her desire for
the cloister, her Superiors felt it wiser to wait. The
Mother Assistant, who came to Neuchâtel to replace
the Superior for the remainder of the year, had a
private talk with each Sister, and at that time
Louisa opened her heart to her. The Mother arranged to have her transferred to a house of the
Society in Reims for a year. There was no school
attached, the house was enclosed and the life was
very regular. Louisa did housework and had much
time for prayer and solitude. It was a time of grace
for her. However, her vows were postponed for another six months because of uncertainty caused by
her continued longing for the cloister.

Her health suffered at Reims because of the work
and the climate. She was given a fortnight's holiday
with the Mother Assistant who had been at
Neuchâtel: "a fortnight in paradise." Finally, on
February 3, 1933, she made her vows. Vows in that
congregation were made for one year and renewed
annually. "I took them forever, and forever..."

Longing to share her faith with those she loved,

Louisa wanted to offer her life for the conversion of her family. The Vicar General of Reims, whom she consulted, told her she could offer herself as a victim to God's will for the salvation of her family, not for their conversion—and not asking to die.

Overwhelmed by the Eucharist, Louisa could not conceive that one could distinguish "salvation" from the plenitude of this privileged meeting with the Lord. In her enthusiasm, she would have wanted her whole family to follow her into the Church and all her friends to join her in the convent!

With wisdom, this priest made her attentive to the mystery of God's calls and to the very diverse paths of souls. If it is true that the truth is in the Church and it is worth the trouble to give one's life so that that would be recognized, it is true also that recognizing this truth is not obtained by reason alone. It presupposes an interior illumination of grace, a free gift of God. To assure the eternal happiness of those that one loves, what is important is to sustain their fidelity to the light received up to the final meeting with God.

Later in Sister Mary's life, Our Lord was to tell her: "It is in the interior of the soul that conversions take place—they are not always visible, but they are—and that for all eternity. Do not doubt any longer. . .Believe—hope—sacrifice yourself; leave them to Me. . .I have My time, and My means are not your means." Also: "The great evil of Protestantism is that it deprives so many souls of goodwill of an immense share of graces obtained through My Passion and which are coveyed to you through the Sacraments. Ah, how it limits My action in souls who do not seek Me further and do not 'follow' Me further because they believe that they have responded definitively to My call once and for all....The great evil of Protestantism is that error wears the mask of truth. Much courage and deep personal labor is needed to discover the mask, to reject it, then to come humbly to the Source of Truth to ask for His light and His strength. *'Let your light shine before men,'* in order that they may understand that your Church is Christ, is the Truth." (No. 288). And: "I shall use you to bring back many Protestants to the Church, and in a way beyond all that you can imagine, because I work as God. It is as God that I keep My promises; it is as God that I am pleased to respond to humble confidence." (No. 14).

Louisa returned to Neuchâtel where she was given a class of very young children to teach. She was very pleased with them, and with the new Superior of the community who gave an example of gentleness, silence and mortification which appealed to Louisa. As she had lost considerable weight at Reims and was still overtired, she suffered a hemorrhage in October and was sent to La Chaux-de-Fonds for several weeks to recuperate. She soon returned to Neuchâtel, where the good care and concern of the Sisters helped her to continue her teaching.

Shortly after renewing her vows on February 3, 1936, she was seated at table with an elderly sister who spoke of her surprise when the Superior of the Hospital Sisters in Neuchâtel left her community to enter the Poor Clares. This astonished Louisa, who thought it was not possible to renounce one's vows. The Sister explained that one could always leave an active order for a more austere one. "It was like a flash of lightning" to Louisa; ". . . in one second I realized that that was what I must do."

Before speaking to anyone else about her conviction, Louisa wanted to consult the Abbé Zundel, a priest noted for his holiness. In spite of many obstacles to their meeting, in an almost miraculous fashion she found herself able to speak with him at his parents' home in Neuchâtel. She told him only of her great desire to go and pray in a convent, not daring to mention the longing of her heart. "Looking at me, he said: 'Poor Clare!' as if it were written on my forehead!" From a Capuchin Father who visited the community at Easter, she obtained information concerning the process of transfer.

Louisa had hoped to leave before the next renewal of her vows. That summer she took part in a long retreat that had been arranged for the young Professed Sisters. The retreat master questioned her closely concerning her vocation and pronounced it a true call from God. Through the influence of Abbé Zundel, Louisa was accepted by the Poor Clares at Evian. She entered on the first of September, 1936.

The community was supported by the needlework of the nuns. Most of the day was spent in a common work-community room, working together. As the only postulant, Louisa ordinarily spoke only to a Sister assigned to her as her "Angel" to help her adjust. There was no Novice Mistress or novitiate. No instructions.

Louisa found her happiness in the long hours spent in prayer, especially after Holy Communion. Other than that, she suffered greatly from the intense cold and the insufficient food. She further stated: "There was a strange conception of the religious life and of spiritual perfection. God, Holy Church, our Superiors were mentioned only with fear—almost with resentment."

Unfortunately, the Abbess at this time was suffering from a serious nervous disorder which prevented her from discharging the duties of her office as she should have. Problems naturally arose.

When an ecclesiastical superior came for a visitation at Christmas time, he spoke to each member of the Community individually, and investigated everything. At the end of the visitation, he told the assembled community that if anyone wished to communicate with him she had the right to do so, a matter which Louisa had asked about when she spoke with him. As a result, Louisa was looked upon with disfavor, and she sensed she was no longer wanted. Just before Easter, she had a hemorrhage and asked her "Angel" if she had to report it. The latter, knowing the community wanted an excuse to send Louisa away, wept, then advised her to ask the chaplain's opinion. He said she should say nothing but to tell the Abbess he had forbidden her to fast.

The Ecclesiastical Superior returned to give an Easter conference, "the only one I heard there," as Louisa later said. When her Superiors denied Louisa permission to speak to him, she wrote a letter and handed it in sealed. This caused trouble— an upset. "Never in all the 40 years I have spent in this house has a single sealed letter been sent out!" Louisa was sent away after being informed that it was "not on account of your health, for with a few readjustments it might still have been possible, but on account of your bad spirit."

It is indeed certain that if Sister Mary of the Trinity had been consulted, she would never have permitted the publication of this painful page of her story. In the account of her conversion-vocation which she gave to her confessor in Jerusalem, she explicitly stated: "If I have written all this, Father, it is of course for you alone, and for the good consuming fire, the symbol of the 'blazing furnace of charity' in which all our troubles will be burned away. . ." This portion of the account was in fact published. Father Silvère, who was responsible for the publication, gave his reasons: "1) because they [the facts] are true, and 2) because we believe that these pages will be read by many religious who will be able to profit from them."

How had this happened? This unfortunate situation at the monastery of Evian was the result of the multiple trials it had undergone since the beginning of the century (expulsion in 1903). One could not accuse the community of relaxation; the life was very austere, poverty most rigorous, the prayer life fervent; on this point, other testimony has confirmed that of Louisa. In spite of the small number of sisters, never was the day or night Office interrupted. But charity seems to have been understood as a long mutual acceptance, which covered the failings with a certain mentality, including the illness and incapacity of the Abbess.

In such an environment, a postulant who had a little personality quickly appeared as a foreign body. Louisa was not the only one to know this sorrow, to be refused or to understand on her own account that she should leave. A Superior of another convent to which Louisa later applied told her that one of her nieces had been mysteriously sent away from Evian. "There is a Mother Superior there who sends her people away—no one knows why."

Louisa did not, however, draw any conclusion about leaving voluntarily or expecting dismissal. In spite of the hardships and her poor health, in spite of the weight of the spiritual climate, she was happy with the long hours of prayer; she was ready to love her Sisters as they were and to do everything to bring about a renewal. For Christmas she had received a little fir tree from her friend Bluette, and she had composed a song to tell her thanks to the community for having been accepted.

"There was an abyss between them and me: education, outlook, the needs of the soul." Louisa was completely unconscious of anything with which they could reproach her. What charge could one make against her? Certainly no fault that could have motivated a dismissal from the community. Yet it is necessary to try to see very loyally what could have provoked such a painful decision, what one can guess through the remarks and reticences of certain statements. These are human miseries, particularly felt in the cloistered religious life, the crucible of charity. These remarks will help one better understand some passages of the Notebooks, for not only at Evian, but already earlier and right up to her death in Jerusalem, Louisa drew upon herself the incomprehension of her fellow Sisters.

First of all, she was very absent-minded, as has already been seen. In the housework, with her feeble strength and her desire to do everything to perfection, she was quickly lost, and that annoyed the good housekeepers who surrounded her. Often Louisa asked questions on points of doctrine or of religious life, questions which did not even come to the minds of persons who were more simple or were born in a Catholic environment. Those who saw in these questions the sign of a critical spirit, in a negative sense, judged her mistakenly. Louisa was an intellectual and a convert. She thirsted for truth and clarity. She asked questions in order to enlighten her own conduct, not to make reproaches to others.

After those dark years, the monastery at Evian knew a new spring. A group of religious from the convent of Versailles, new Superiors, completely renewed the community. Vocations were manifested, such as Sister Mary of the Trinity had hoped for, and Evian was even able to participate in a missionary foundation.

On March 27, 1965, a little group of Poor Clares left the monastery to establish themselves at La Plaine (Geneva) as a first stake of a return of the Poor Clares to the French-speaking part of Switzerland. Since then, this little religious family has settled in the area of Vaud, at Jongny, in the parish of Vevey. The law forbidding the foundation of new convents in Switzerland having been abrogated, the realization of this great desire of Sister Mary of the Trinity is now possible.

Louisa wrote, "You understand better now the intensity of the longing which I have been given for a small convent, quite poor and new, in my country, with two aims: to oppose Protestantism, and to establish a community in which the Holy Rule will be lived in its Gospel simplicity." Our Lord was to tell her, "Ah, if all My religious, all those who exercise responsibility in My Church had lived the Truth professed by their lips, the schisms which rend My Church would not exist."

Louisa had left Evian on April 10, 1937, feeling that she had lost her vocation, fearing it was her own fault. "It was as if everything had been torn out of my soul..." Several days before, during Exposition of the Blessed Sacrament, the Voice which she had already heard, though rarely, spoke within her soul. "Let Me direct things," He said. When Louisa asked what she should give Him, He replied: "You will suffer." "That," Louisa remarked simply, "is what I carried away with me from Evian."

She only passed through Lausanne, this time to consult Doctoress Olivier and to send a call to Countess Agliardi. When she learned that the Abbè Zundel was preaching a retreat at the nearby town of Morges, she went there. Three days after leaving Evian, she found refuge in the home of a childhood friend at Morges, Miss Marie Henrioud. Bluette, who was notified, also telephoned her, and on the 17th, Louisa sent her this card: "...excellent visit to Doctoress Olivier. Result: nothing bad, no danger, a simple recommendation of extra nutrition, pills to remedy the anemia, then avoid fasts. I will therefore be quickly on my feet again and ready to return according to providential indication. This morning, it is just a week since I left Evian."

The retreat did her much good, especially as the Abbé Zundel gave her to understand that he believed in her vocation. But where? Later, when Louisa had experienced the inner voice of Jesus, she asked Him why He had not sent her someone to guide her along the way; He responded: "You had to discover My Voice alone by your own efforts, by stripping yourself. No one else could have made you hear it. Now that I speak to you freely, you need a Father to control your decisions and your thoughts. If only you understood this gift of My Mercy! It has been My will that divine help should reach you through human means—those means are surrendered to your free initiative—do you understand your dignity?"

At the end of the retreat, Louisa found a position near Lausanne with a working-class family of six children whose mother was in the hospital. The filth and disorder were inconceivable (Louisa had not known of these conditions), and the illness of the mother was one that demanded extreme cleanliness to prevent contagion. The work was too hard for Louisa, and the doctor spoke of putting her into the hospital. The Countess Agliardi once more came to her aid. She was looking for a companion for her convalescent elder son. It would mean a stay at Cortina d'Ampezzo, a health resort in the Italian Tyrol. Louisa had the fresh air she needed, and could attend Mass every day in that Catholic area. From there, she traveled in Italy with the family, and accompanied the Countess wherever she went for the next three months. All the while she continued applying to any convent that offered any possibility of acceptance. She was refused everywhere because of her former vows, her age (she was now 36) and the lack of a dowry.

While still at Cortina d'Ampezzo, Louisa received a letter from Alice saying that she and her family were planning to come to Switzerland for the summer, and then she and her children would go on to the Transvaal to see her father and the other members of the family. Believing that Louisa was still at Evian, Alice said she would visit her there, and expressed her great desire that Louisa could accompany her to Africa.

In July, the whole Agliardi family emigrated to the mountains, at Santa Caterina, near the Passo dello Stelvio. It was from there that Louisa informed her friend, Bluette, on July 20th: "Alice has been at Yverdon since the beginning of the month. Her husband permits her to continue her trip with Viviane and Charly to Elim in order to see Papa again. I am going to answer their request to accompany Alice and to go meet them. Since there is no possibility here of entering a monastery, if I am supposed to remain in the world, there is no reason I should live far away from them. Papa is offering me a round trip ticket good for a year. He writes me with such goodness, even foreseeing that I will be able to busy myself teaching with the Belgian religious to whom he spoke of me. We are thinking of leaving at the end of August."

Louisa feared she was taking back the offering she had previously made to God of her affection and desire for her family. She looked for some sign of His will. The Countess urged her not to disappoint her family. The Abbé Zundel advised her to go and "take a rest in the affection of [her] family, while bringing them His," and he added that if the call of God persisted thereafter, "He will surely open for you the convent that will be your refuge." That is exactly what happened.

The departure was precipitous. On August 10, she informed Bluette: "Our departure has been set suddenly and irrevocably for the 12th of August. Departure from Genoa (on the steamer 'Giulio Cesare')...I therefore will not be returning to Switzerland. It costs me dearly to leave. However, I think it is the will of Our Lord...perhaps He will accord me there what I have not found here. I don't know, and what's the difference for me provided He be served and loved."

The reunion was a joyful one. The family had not been together since 1920 when the Jaques family had gone to Switzerland for a holiday. Through three letters addressed to Bluette, we have a few details on Louisa's stay in South Africa.

Louisa wrote: "I could have remained in the home of Zabeth because she needs at least one person to help her for a while. With their consent, I seized on the run the chance to have a job as a French teacher with a family in Johannesburg." She related the devotion of her brother Alexander and her sister-in-law Lucy: "...they do a lot for the blacks and are loved by them...they house at their own expense about 10 blacks who could not pay their tuition. They really have the missionary spirit." And this charming anecdote: "Alex has many misadventures with the poor missionary automobile which loses parts all along the road. They almost did not arrive in time to say good-bye to Alice because of a breakdown that lasted two hours. Pierrette kept saying: 'Jesus, make it cease stopping!' And one of her more practical little cousins said: 'You are stupid! It is not Jesus, don't you see it is the motor?' We have no misunderstandings, no discussions, no difficulty among us, tenderness on seeing each other again, respect for convictions and personal liberty.

What can one do to SAY that in spite of everything, all religions are not equal?"

Louisa also spoke of her foreboding of an upheaval in that country: "If you saw how in general people permit themselves to treat the blacks. We will have merited it when their revolt comes. It causes me such pain to see that they forget that Jesus relives and asks to be reborn in *each* creature. It is His call that the souls reveal without knowing it and which one can perceive everywhere, everywhere, everywhere; it is tragic. To show Him, to make Him loved, what an immense apostolate!"

Alice and her children sailed for America on September 30, 1937. Louisa accompanied her as far as Johannesburg. A Belgium missionary she had met on the steamer to Africa had told her that there were only two convents of contemplative nuns in South Africa, the Carmelites in Johannesburg and the Capuchin Nuns in Melville. He had recommended her to the Carmelites, and Louisa used this trip to visit the community and make application. She had also obtained a position as governess in a Johannesburg family so she could earn enough money either to respond to her vocation, or pay for her return to Europe.

Acceptance into Carmel was delayed because the monastery at Evian did not send the required testimonial letter. By the time she received a favorable reply from the Carmel at Johannesburg, Louisa had lost her courage, and had begun arrangements to return to Switzerland with a journey to Jerusalem on the way. She wrote: "I must have lost my vocation because it [the acceptance by Carmel] gives me no joy. I feel no attraction—it leaves me indiffer-

ent. Whereas, if it were from the Poor Clares, I would
run to them...I thought of stopping in Jerusalem,
taking a position in some family—trying out the climate and enquiring whether the Poor Clares, either
in that city or elsewhere, would accept me...I no
longer have the love nor the desire for a life of continual restraint—except for that of the Poor Clares;
I do not know why; I have loved them and have
wanted to share their life ever since the moment
when by chance I first heard about them." Louisa
had read about the Poor Clares in Jerusalem in a
biography of Father Charles de Foucauld. A Belgian
priest had given her their address, which she used
in obtaining the visa for her passport.

When she had earned the necessary fare, Louisa
returned to her family for a three-week visit. At the
end of the visit, she told them she was planning
to return to Europe. Her father was heart-broken,
fearing that she was going to enter another convent. Louisa denied this, for she felt that her vocation had already been lost. In fact, she was already
in the process of arranging for a position as governess with a family in the Tyrol. When she mentioned
that she intended to visit Jerusalem on her way to
Europe, her family's opposition vanished. They even
insisted on giving her money for her pilgrimage, and
her father advised her to cancel her plans to enter
service with the family in the Tyrol. They wanted
her to return to them in Africa.

Louisa left South Africa at the end of May and
arrived in Jerusalem on June 24, 1938. The next
day she visited the Poor Clare monastery, Our Lady
of Sion, and was praying in the chapel when an extern Sister, Sister Angela, came up to her. The Sister

inquired if Louisa wanted to become a Poor Clare. The interview with the Abbess, Mother Amandine, followed. "The Blessed Sacrament said nothing—He said absolutely nothing to me. But my heart was weeping."

3

IN THE HARBOR
(1938 - 1940)

"I did not have the courage. He gave it to me...
He has always given me everything...eight days
later, on June 30, 1938, I entered."

"We well remember that entrance into the cloister," wrote a former Superior of the Poor Clares in
Jerusalem, "as if it had taken place this very day.
On the evening of June 30, 1938, the two heavy doors
closed on the new arrival, who was never to leave
again... The candidate seemed a little frightened
to find herself among these religious with their veils
lowered to come to the door of the cloister. After
the chanting of the *Te Deum* in the choir, there was
the reception in the chapter. Everyone was
astonished. The religious were struck by the sight
of this person who was so thin and so sad, dressed
in very high heels, and who, with a brusque gesture, almost a violent one, threw her felt hat down
in order to receive the black bonnet of the postulants.
The majority of the young Sisters smiled, others remained serious, a few cried with emotion. None had
the expression of the one whom the Reverend Mother
had just named Sister Mary of the Trinity. When
she came to give the kiss of peace to each Sister,
her face expressed fear, almost terror, as if she had
been buried alive. Later, the Sisters realized why..."

It was anguish over the future. She was in the harbor. But it was not the first time she had docked there. She had been there before, and they had nevertheless shoved her out again to the open sea of the world. She had to go through the testing of the postulancy and then the novitiate: two years of uncertainty. Still more profoundly, she carried in her subconscious the terror of the cloister. These cloistered nuns who received her, happy in their monastery, could not guess it. Nevertheless it was there that the Lord called her, and there only where she could find, with His grace, peace and joy.

The new arrival was entrusted to a mistress to whom she showed herself to be very open, and to a "good angel," that is to say to another postulant who had been in the monastery eight months longer but who was ten years younger. Very humbly, the little postulant who was past 37 years old began meekly learning about the life of a Poor Clare. Between the two postulants, both of frail health and deprived of a mother since birth, the most fraternal intimacy developed.

Though endowed with great originality, the new sister tried not to be noticed. She was less frightened than on the day of her entrance, but her expressive face often reflected a profound sadness, of which the sisters did not know the cause; to themselves they thought: "She must have suffered greatly."

Only the Mother Abbess and her council knew of her Protestant origins and her first tries at religious life. For the community as a whole, sympathy succeeded astonishment. They were struck by her gentleness, by her desire to adapt to the common life and her attention to rendering with delicacy many little favors.

In the heart of the postulant was a quieting and hope. In her first letters addressed from the monastery, she announced her joy.

On September 2, 1938, to Bluette: "You will be very happy about the grace Jesus has given me. June 30, I entered the Poor Clares here. They greeted me with so much joy and charity, without a dowry, nothing but my unappeased desire to serve Our Lord finally." She added this remark which softened her judgment of Evian: ". . . here, there is a different spirit. Perhaps it is because my disposition is less demanding; what bothered me before has become sweetness and joy. Everything is grace. I am thankful for having passed by Evian, and so happy, so happy here. . ."

Upon entering the monastery, she had loyally informed the Reverend Mother of her state of health, without hiding anything of her long illness nor of her relapses. On both sides, they agreed to have confidence in the Lord and to attempt a trial of this austere life. This confidence seems to have been answered. For four years, Sister Mary of the Trinity did not spend a day in the infirmary; they never saw her stretched out on a chaise-lounge, and the fever which carried her off was her first illness in the convent. But it was at the price of so many precautions, so much energy, and such support of grace!

The other Sisters, not having passed through such physical and mental trials, scarcely suspected how much effort the life in community could demand of Sister Mary of the Trinity. Her courage and long training permitted her to hide her suffering. She was also strengthened by the inner Voice which asked: "Make Me a present of. . .all weariness, suffering, that others will never guess, and which you will hide, to prove your love to Me and because I have such need of your gifts!" (Note No. 3).[1] To see her going to common work, light and joyous, more sprightly than the young ones, how could one think that she always felt fragile, at the mercy of the least cold weather? She was living her Morning Offering: ". . .Here are my hands and feet that You may make them agile, that You may rivet them to Your service. . ." Many times, however, when she was exhausted, the cough would begin again.

By taste, Sister Mary of the Trinity would have preferred to remain always in her cell and do little chores, a book open in front of her. But the Superiors thought the open air would do her good. They also made her understand that the others did without reading during work hours. Our Lord Himself encouraged her with these words spoken after the Consecration of the Mass: "Do you understand how obedient I am? I give Myself, I submit to the desires of all. Do the same. Mother Vicaress wishes you to go more quickly to the garden: please her. Your Superior wishes you to be as little as possible in your cell, submit. . .what does it matter to you whether you are here or there! I accompany you everywhere." (No. 119). From then on, she tried to take part in the work of the monastery with ready generosity to the point of acquiring an adaptability which her beginnings would not have let one suspect.

The refectory was for her a constant occasion of renouncements. They had allowed her a few dispensations in the beginning, but later and especially after her profession, Sister Mary wanted to keep to the common regime in everything. She even added to the frugality of the menu many mortifications known to Jesus alone and at times suggested by Him: "Now that your health has improved, you can allow your good appetite some little mortifications. At every meal faithfully offer Me some little portion you can do without, for those who are dying of hunger." (No. 160). And again: "At the evening meal, give Me for others who suffer the dried fruit you can do without. Will you...?" (No. 618). Many of these small denials were scarcely guessed at by a few of the religious.

Getting up for the midnight Office was very hard on her, especially in winter. When would she go to sleep after Matins? They had given her a cell on the sunny side of the building, but winter nights are very cold in Jerusalem, particularly at the monastery, which is situated on the heights. After three or four nights, they told the Sister to rest. Later her health would allow her to rise for Matins several nights each week. Jesus approved this and encouraged her: "Your Superior is right in telling you to endeavor to come to the Rosary four nights. [During the war years Matins could not be recited at midnight because of the imposed blackout. To be faithful to the custom of night rising, the Sisters prayed the Rosary at that time.] It is in order that you should pray also at night that I have wished you to be My Poor Clare. What do you fear? I will help you." (No. 82).

At times Our Lord Himself urged Sister Mary of the Trinity to partially renounce the dispensation granted to her: "Come to Matins four nights in succession. I will give you the strength." (No. 566). He

SR. MARY OF THE HOLY TRINITY 79

also made promises—and kept them: "If tonight you take the place at Matins of those who have colds, I will keep you from catching it." (No. 587). Sister Mary of the Trinity *alone* escaped the influenza which attacked the community! When she wished to obtain a great grace, she asked permission to make what she called a "novena" of Matins, a very great effort for her. A short while before her death, when she felt the first effects of the illness which was to carry her off, she made one of these novenas for her Aunt Alice. To a Sister who was surprised to see her every night in choir, in spite of her state of fatigue, she said with emotion: "It is for the repose of the soul of my 'Little Mother.'"

The year of postulancy went by. Convinced of her good disposition and judging her to be of sufficient strength, the Superiors admitted her to the noviti-ate. She received the habit on August 28, 1939, Saint Augustine's day. How well Sister Mary of the Trinity must have understood his words: "You have made us for Thyself, O Lord, and our heart is not at rest until it rests in Thee." As heroic as her quest for the Lord had been up to then, her heart still did not know the perfect repose of being next to Him. She kept a tendency to expect from the creatures around her a comprehension and affection that they could not give. This year of novitiate, which she confided to the maternal protection of the Virgin Mary, was not a simple formality but a time of intense spiritual growth.

To this period belong the first written Notes when Jesus called her "My little fiancee." The spiritual principles He placed before her would be repeated over and again and amplified. "Forget yourself! Do

not occupy yourself with your spiritual or material
needs. When you have all that is necessary, you deprive Me of the joy of taking care of you." (No. 1).
"Do not defend yourself. Set no value on your rights.
Let Me have the pleasure of defending you at the
right time. Be silent, silent...as I am." (No. 2).
"Kindness...Indulgence...Keep your soul free and
transparent, above the troubles, cares and misunderstandings which the cloister produces... Teach,
only by example. Silence, silence in the Heart of your
God." (No. 4).

Sister Mary of the Trinity remained in good health
and even seemed to get stronger, so the community
found no difficulty in admitting her to profession.
The first profession of a religious is for a limited
time. If the Community and the Sister agree that
the commitment should be made permanent, she
makes her final vows. On August 29, 1940, Sister
Mary pronounced her vows for three years; but in
her heart, she was giving herself to God for always,
not daring to hope for three more years of life.

The day of her profession was more one of Heaven
than of earth. She did not tell her secret, but her
Sisters had only to see her to sense it. She herself
wrote in the story of her conversion: "The evening
of my first vows, He told me that He was pleased.
He said it three times. That is all that has filled
my life since then: that He should be pleased!" On
September 2, she recorded the words spoken to her
on that joyous day of her Profession: "You are
Mine—you are altogether Mine...Do not go away.
Stay with Me, *in* Me who never leave you. I have
waited so long for you. This is the only reality: *I
love you and I take care of you.* And that is for now

and for eternity. Everything else must be borne with meekness and patience. They are only fleeting shadows which pass around you. But I remain. I love you and I take care of you." (No. 5). There is already a hint of a particular plan, a special vocation for Sister Mary of the Trinity: "I am *happy* because you have come at last. I await many others like yourself in My Church, in My house. To attract them, do all that I tell you." (No. 8).

All day long she wore, as is the custom, the crown of roses which made her look so young. She had exchanged the white veil of the novice for the black one of the professed nun, which did not make her look older at all but gave her a more serious expression. Since she had been wearing the holy habit, she seemed several years younger; the head-band covered the wrinkles in her forehead.

On that day, the Church celebrates the martyrdom of Saint John the Baptist, "friend of the (divine) Spouse." Somebody told her that this coincidence was probably an invitation to silent suffering, known only to God. She closed her eyes a moment and did not answer.

Was one source of silent suffering that of seeming to be kept deliberately in the background? One of the Notes seems to indicate this: "They try to hide you, to ignore your existence; it is well." (No. 14). To understand this it must be remembered that Sister Mary of the Trinity had many talents which inevitably brought her to the fore and could have made a star of her. Her Superiors acted wisely in avoiding public occasions of notice, but it may have given the Sister an impression of displeasure which naturally caused her suffering. Nevertheless, for feast days, surmounting her timidity, she composed poems or a song or drew pictures to please her Superiors and Sisters.

Thus for Christmas in 1940, this poem dedicated:

> To our Good Mother
> Thanking her for the trouble
> She took to save
> a vocation.
> The Infant Jesus gives thanks!

In Bethlehem there was no such pretty greenery,
heaps of dust and straw; from the straw
hung long cobwebs
waving in the night breeze...
Earth appeared hard and desolate to Me,
however I was happy,
since right next to Me, full of light,
I saw the two eyes of My Mother.
The shepherds came with their presents,
the Wise Men also, then other people.
They placed like relics
what they seemed to have that was best,
some useful or magnificent objects.
I smiled...but I had without saying it
...nobody guessed it—a desire!
I dreamt of holding in My little hands...a rose,
in full bloom, without thorns, fully open or
    half-closed
with transparent petals, supple as desired
to offer it like a large flower fallen from Heaven
to My Mother or to make it My rattle...
Be blessed, you who have near My crib

in your home finally placed the fresh rose,
the rose which I awaited: make it beautiful
Your darling, My Christmas rose.

On those feast days did she experience a certain
indifference as to the use of her talents or a prudent counsel to be humble, as if she desired to be
ignored or hide herself? The inner Word gave her
peace: "Bury yourself in My Heart, and let Me act."
(No. 14). It is in the Heart of the Lord that she must
"bury her life" like the seed in the earth so that
it will bear abundant fruit.

Sentences such as: "What does it matter to you
if they do not want you in this house, provided I
want you here and am pleased with you" (No. 48)
or: "Perhaps you will not be much loved by your
Sisters and Superiors—what does it matter?" (No.
70) convey a sense of conflict, of misunderstandings.
Are we to conclude that the Sister underwent some
persecution? Certainly not. Outside of the few inevitable misunderstandings, she found a profound
understanding among her Superiors, who watched
over her with great solicitude. Nevertheless, we can
say that she was not always understood by some Sisters who, at times, showed her some antipathy.

Let us remember that Saint Therese of the Child
Jesus did not always have the sympathy of all her
Sisters!

Not content with words of comfort: "Am I not
enough for you? Is it not sufficient for you to know
that your Jesus loves you?" (No. 49), like the excellent Teacher that He is, Our Lord reminded Sister
Mary of the Trinity that such small misunderstandings are inevitable in the very close situation

of the cloister, "but those who love Me take no notice of them. Your real Cloister. . . is My Heart." (No. 47). Here she will be given "joy, strength, meekness, love. For I wish you to be joyous, and strong, irresistibly loving—and very meek." "Ask Me for two graces for the common life: to be indulgent with others, 'letting the tares grow with the good grain,' the strength silently on every occasion, without relaxing, to overcome evil by good." (No. 52). That Sister Mary of the Trinity used these principles to shape her life, that this opposition brought out her charity and humility is attested by a Superior who wrote soon after the Sister's death: ". . .the contradictions in the midst of which she lived here brought out better her patience and her forgetfulness of self."

Since January 1st of that year, Sister did not put any date on her Notes; she only rarely indicated any. It was at the request of her confessor that in the last months of her life she gave more dates. It is due to the loyalty with which Sister Mary of the Trinity reported in her Notebooks the warnings perceived within, and thanks also to the sincerity of the testimony of her fellow Sisters, that we can follow the progress of grace in her. These words of counsel are also a warning for us; they reveal to us the demands of this interior listening.

What did she still have to learn? In the first place, that total *poverty* which consists of renouncing our own will. Material poverty did not seem to have cost her much. It answered that profound desire which had drawn her to Saint Clare. "Poverty for us, Poor Clares, consists especially in not losing time," she would say. She had learned its value from Jesus: "When you waste your time, you do Me an injury;

you treat My gifts with contempt, the *present* that I surrender to your love and to your generosity." (No. 23). If she was rather slow at work, it was not for want of zeal, but she did very well what she had to do, and she put forth the same effort in accomplishing the most crude or the most minute work. Her listening heart would learn the secret harmony governing the use of time: "Do not tire of asking for Love: it transforms everything. Even time: thus when one loves much, one has plenty of time, time in which to do many things. When you love more, you will be less slow, work will slip through your fingers. Do not stop loving Me for a minute!" (No. 359).

On the other hand, learning interior poverty was a hard battle for her. What struck others about Sister Mary of the Trinity was her great energy, her self-possession, let us say her will. She was not in the cloister by attraction, still less by sentiment, but by an act of the will. She remained there up to the end in spite of interior conflicts that only God knew about, by a constant effort sustained by grace. Certain of the Notes reveal discreetly these temptations against her vocation: "If you stay here with Me you will do good here—but without seeing it. The deeper the good, the less apparent it is. If you remain here, you will do something for Me— with Me." (No. 202). Also, God uses others to sanctify us. Sister Mary of the Trinity, so complex and so willful, probably would never have arrived at this perfection of charity without the help of religious life and particularly of the cloistered life. She was very conscious that she had been brought to the Poor Clares by a merciful plan of the Lord. "Dear God,

thank You for having given me Sisters and Superiors
to snatch my poor soul away from idleness, egoism,
pride." (No. 629).

She wanted to follow her Lord, "meek and humble of heart." She acquired gentleness at the price
of long and patient efforts. The vivacity of certain
retorts, the little pranks which escaped from her—
rarely—toward her Mothers, who loved her and
showed themselves to be indulgent, let one understand well enough the struggles she sustained. Little by little, the ardor of the combat against herself
grew softer to the point where most of the Sisters
scarcely suspected the persevering efforts of this soul,
who was resolved to conquer herself whatever the
cost. At the end of her life, this vigilance over herself was constant.

Another form of interior poverty that she had to
discover was the silence of the cloister. This was a
great penance for her, since she would have liked
to show her affection, to be understood. Very expansive and spontaneous, she would often have liked
to express her attention to others or her interest
in a reading selection or a piece of work. She
received this enlightenment: "There are many things
that you might tell your Sisters and that I wish
you to communicate to them: but I wish you to speak
to them by your silence; that will be your way of
passing on My messages. It is sufficient *to be.*" (No.
282). It was necessary to accustom her patiently to
this work on herself. One of the Mothers, to whom
she had permission to talk, obliged her to do so only
rarely, when she really needed an explanation or
a favor, which happened often, for Sister Mary of
the Trinity was very meticulous. The novice bent

herself to this discipline and on each meeting answered with a smile, keeping herself from uttering a useless word, even if it seemed justified to her. After her last retreat, finished on December 8, 1941, she assured this Mother that she had now "understood silence," and since then she acted accordingly.

One of the old nuns of the monastery and a former Superior, with whom the Sister had sometimes worked, wrote on September 15, 1944: "About that time I well remember saying to her, 'Why do you always go up to the older Sisters and begin to speak to them? You should wait until they speak to you and then answer them amiably. That is what we were always taught in the novitiate and it is the custom.' She was ever after faithful to this injunction." Jesus manifested His approval, and indicated the response He looked for with these words: "It is not for you to forestall your Sisters [in the sense of speaking first], but when they come to you, always welcome them with meekness and cheerfulness." (No. 592).

One can also imagine how hard *obedience* was for her, who declared herself "extremely independent." Independent and, having the faults of her qualities, obstinate and tenacious in her decisions. In the world, nobody could make her give way if she judged herself to be in the right. In the cloister, obedience rendered her flexible, but at the price of many efforts and of what fidelity to interior grace! We have the echo of these struggles in her Notes: "Do you realize that you are *nothing*? Apart from Me you are nothing but rebellion, refusal, negation." (No. 29). "Do you understand now how unhappy you are when you refuse to give Me what I ask of you? I ask you through the wishes of your Superiors and Sisters. Pay attention to them. Never refuse a request. That still happens too often." (No. 30). "You are not yet perfectly obedient; often you do not leave everything at the first sound of the bell. Respond more quickly to My Voice. . ." (No. 58).

These warnings must describe well what must have been her first movements. However, the Mother Abbess, like the Mistress of Novices, affirmed that Sister Mary of the Trinity was perfectly obedient. Not only did she submit to her Superiors, but she also showed herself to be comprehending and receptive of her Sisters' wishes, always ready to be of service. "You did well in submitting to your little Sister even though you had an excellent reason for not obeying her. I am pleased! I speak to you through the lips of others; even if they do not always say exactly what I desire, it is always I who am asking for a sign of love. Obey them with the same love you have for Me." (No. 41).

These remarks on her interior struggles should not mislead us about her true comportment in the cloister. We can do no better than to quote the conclusion of the testimony of one of her Superiors: "It was definitely her gentleness, her attention to others and her desire to efface herself which most impressed her Sisters."

For Sister Mary of the Trinity, the practice of the vows blossomed into a *profound and expansive charity.* It manifested itself in kindly attention for all the Sisters, respect for her Superior and a great deference for the aged Sisters. Her charity was ingenious and did not end with nice words. If Mother Mistress, who was the infirmarian, needed to relieve a sick religious, Sister Mary of the Trinity, who had much practical knowledge, would suggest a simple and effective remedy. If a Sister neglected some wound, she would worry about it and would advise some medication. She was always available to watch over a sick religious, and when a younger Sister was tired, without paying attention to her own weakness, she offered to "replace" her at Matins. During the last weeks of the illness of a jubilarian Sister, Sister Mary of the Trinity showed her all the delicacy in her heart, trying to find every means of comforting her. A little later, she showed proof of the same devotion during the illness of the Mistress of Novices, for whom she always showed the liveliest thankfulness.

She had certain gestures all her own. A Sister who was immobilized as a result of a fall was supposed to remain stretched out in the open air. Passing by, Sister Mary of the Trinity would kiss the sick foot, as if the Sister would be relieved by this gesture.

Certain virtues grew in her during those years spent in the cloister, but from the first day her spirituality, which was profound and without ostentation, was the edification of her fellow Sisters. One felt that she carefully prepared herself for prayer and the reception of the Sacraments. One Sister remarked that each time, when beginning the Office, she seemed collected and radiant with happiness. Severe with herself in this service of the praise of the Lord, she permitted herself in this domain to make friendly reproaches to the others for their little negligences. "You look like you are convalescing!" she would say to a young Sister in front of her, who let herself go and leaned on the choir stall during Office.

The article of the Creed, "I believe in the Communion of Saints," had been a revelation for her. In every circumstance, she implored the prayers of her fellow Sisters; for her part she prayed fervently for the souls in Purgatory and entrusted to them her most pressing intentions. But her devotion went first to the Holy Virgin Mary, then to Saint Francis of Assisi and to Saint Clare. Having learned that Saint Colette, the reformer of the Order, had passed through several different houses before being fixed in her vocation, she considered her as a particular protectress; she would say: "That happened to the great saints. They searched for their way in several communities and came there where God wanted them." It is revealing to see the dependence of a prayer left by Sister Mary of the Trinity on one of Saint Colette. The saint gave herself to the work of renewal of the Franciscan Order to which the Lord called her with the following prayer. The prayer of Sister Mary of the Trinity contains identical phrases and sentiments.

DEDICATION PRAYER
OF SAINT COLETTE

"O blessed Jesus! I dedicate myself to You in health, in illness, in my life, in my death, in all my desires, in all my deeds, so that I may never work henceforth except for Your glory, and for that for which You have chosen me. From this moment on, dearest Lord, there is nothing which I am not prepared to undertake for love of You."

PRAYER OF SISTER
MARY OF THE TRINITY

"Jesus! I abandon myself for health, for illness, for life, for death, in all my desires, in all my conduct, to work henceforth only for Your glory, for the salvation of souls, for the return of Protestants to the Church. There is nothing henceforth that I do not want to undertake for love of You. Saint Colette, our Mother, help me!"

The final phrase of the prayer by Sister Mary of the Trinity is an explicit acknowledgement of its source. Does it not likewise reveal the Sister's sense of also being chosen for a special work, of having been given a particular vocation?

She had read during her novitiate the *Spiritual Writings* of Charles de Foucauld. No book, she said, had done her more good, and from then on a sort of fraternal intimacy was established between her and the hermit of the Poor Clares of Jerusalem. She had adopted the simple method of prayer of "Brother Charles." " 'What do You have to tell me, oh God? As for me, here's what I have to tell You.' Don't talk any more, look at the Beloved."

Already at Neuchâtel a desire for voluntary mortifications had revealed itself in Louisa. Drawn on by grace, Sister Mary of the Trinity continued to seek supplementary mortification. "Because I love you I have given you a desire to do penance and the strength to do penance." (No. 335). However, these penances were always with the consent of her superior and of her confessor, as is revealed in certain of the Notes. "You may offer Me this little extra penance daily for that intention—if your Father al-

lows it. It is the obedience and love with which you
contrive to offer Me your penances that moves Me."
(No. 42).

Her confessor commented: "Certain persons may
be curious to know whether the Sister practiced extraordinary penances. Yes, as far as she was allowed.
Her confessor always had to restrain her in the use
of small chains and other instruments of penance.
She was especially drawn to the use of thorny
branches in order to make herself suffer." Our Lord
Himself explained the value of such acts: "It is your
self-denial that will tell you whether you love Me—
it is that which will obtain the increase of love that
you desire." (No. 621). How this is accomplished is
further explained: "Your corporal penances please
Me, however small they may be, in the measure in
which they help you to master, together with your
body, your mind, your imagination, your memory,
your will, in order to give them to Me, to place them
in My Heart, where they will find all they need.
Apart from Me, you truly waste them. Am I not sufficient for you? And when these penances are acts
of love asking pardon. . ." (No. 147). Here the sentence is left unfinished through the call of obedience,
a small act of penance which was often required of
Sister Mary of the Trinity and to which she was
faithful, as the Notes bear witness!

Later in this book the general concepts of spiritual
victimhood, especially that consecrated by vow, are
outlined. Excerpts from the Notes expressly present
victimhood as shown in *The Spiritual Legacy of Sister Mary of the Holy Trinity* (see also the Index to
The Spiritual Legacy, pp. 363-364). Nonetheless it

will be advantageous to trace the call to victimhood
in the life of Sister Mary of the Trinity. Not to do
so would be to overlook a crucial element of her life
story and vocation.

As the year of 1941 opened, the Sister was already
asked: "Does this offering frighten you? But it was
in order that you should make it that I have led
you here, even to this hour. . . You are free; but you
will not have given Me everything until the offering has been made in the way I desire it. . ." (No.
21). The same insistence is found much later in the
year in almost identical words: "It is in order that
you should make Me this offering that I have
brought you here, and that I have preserved you all
your life long." (No. 101). It seems that the major
work of this year was that of raising Sister Mary
of the Trinity to the spiritual caliber which would
enable her to make, and to live, such an offering.

By early October, the Lord's invitation to make
this Vow of Victim became more insistent. She
opened her soul about it to her confessor. At his request, she gave him a page of her Notes with this
little letter:

"+Jesus!
From the Monastery of the Poor Clares in Jerusalem—21 October, 1941.

Father,
Here is the little piece of paper you asked for. You
understand why I want this Vow of Victim which
Superiors sometimes permit one to offer to the Lord.

He told me last winter: 'The Saints attracted many
souls to My Church just by the radiance of their

sanctity. You cannot do that, but give yourself and I will use you to attract many souls to the Church. It is I who will do that. But give Me all.' (No. 36).

When I think of our poor life and of the great difficulties which await us, not because of the religious life, but because of the deformations of the religious life, I don't have the courage...

Before I spoke to Reverend Mother about it last summer, because I didn't dare, He told me: 'There is a reason why I ask that of you which you will understand later.'

Since then, silence on the subject. He does not ask in a formal manner, but He has a manner so discreet and so sure of making one understand what He wants that the doubts go away and it is irresistible. I find Him in my poor soul infinitely greater, more delicate than anything I could have imagined...

One can refuse Him nothing.

If I am mistaken, my mistake will only be in trying to be generous, then God will have pity. But it is you who will judge, Father, and I will obey you.

I thank you from the bottom of my heart, Father, and desire to remain always in Him, although unworthily, one of your poor children.

Sister Mary of the Trinity, O.S.C."

The page from the Sister's Notes consisted of the following:

" 'All disorder arises from not listening to the Church. People wish to live outside My Church, although I am there, I who am Source and Strength...

'And those who are in the Church forget to listen

to Me.

'They look on Me as a master, I who am always, unwearyingly at your service, answering your prayers, waiting, hoping that you will ask of Me the better gifts.'

'When I incline toward you, My justice and My Holiness hide themselves; there is only My boundless love calling for yours, giving you confidence, hoping for your generosity.

'Leave all to be wholly Mine, to love Me as a God, as a Saviour, deserves to be loved.

'Listen to Me and look...

'Do you understand...? (No. 63).

'There are several kinds of charity:

'that of the good Samaritan who dresses the wounds of body and soul,

'that which forestalls wounds by being on the watch to do on all occasions to others what we would wish them to do to us,

'but the highest charity is interior charity, which immerses itself in God and is only occupied in revealing Him and making Him known; it is that which sets souls free, that they may of themselves come to Me who give consolation and strength and life.

'There are several kinds of goodwill:

'that which gives Me your works,

'that which gives Me your liberty, your will,

'that which unites itself to My sufferings, that offers itself also as a victim to participate in the expiation of sins. That is the goodwill of My friends, of My intimate friends.

'My love for you is so great that it could not be better expressed than through suffering. Therefore they, too, love Me.

'Do you understand that?

'Do you see how much I have loved you? How I have waited for you, and how I still wait?' (No. 61).

"After that He was silent. But when He is silent, it is as if He still spoke. He makes you understand. To try to tell about it in words is like a caricature. So. . . pardon!"

The confessor assured the Sister of his support and encouraged her to write down these interior words and to submit them to him regularly.

On October 31, Vigil of the Feast of All Saints, the Sister was instructed to ask her Superiors' consent "because you belong to your community." Once the Vow of Victim is pronounced, that person "is entirely delivered up to the good pleasure of God, whatever may be her obligations to her community." (No. 80).

"Do what I tell you without fear," the Sister was told on November 25. "I will be with you." (No. 122). At this time she went to her Superior to ask permission to make the Vow of Victim. She obtained this in such an unexpected way that she could only attribute it to a special help from Our Lord. Father Silvère also interpreted this almost unhoped for consent of her Superior, so readily given, as the sign promised by Our Lord. Jesus Himself would recall that favorable answer as a proof of the fidelity of His word.

It had been announced to Sister Mary of the Trinity: "You will pronounce the Vow of Victim between the hands of My Mother, Mediatrix of all Graces—it is she who will present your offering to God." (No. 110). The expression used by Our Lord:

"You will pronounce the Vow of Victim *between the hands of My Mother...*" manifests a touching detail for a religious of Saint Clare. On the day of her profession she places her joined hands within the open hands of her Abbess and thus pronounces her vows. This overtone must certainly have given joy to the heart of Sister Mary of the Trinity.

As the community entered into a period of retreat on November 29 before the Feast of the Immaculate Conception, the Sister spent these days in intensified preparation.

With what fervor then must not the Sister have pronounced her Vow of Victim on the Feast of the Immaculate Conception, December 8, 1941. Her formula of consecration is not known. She carried it always on her, and she was buried with it. Father Silvère commented regretfully that it was thus buried "without our knowledge."

On this day the Sister noted the following communication: "Henceforth your prayers will obtain conversions because My Mother and yours, Mary— Mediatrix of all Graces—will offer them in union with her own. Rejoice! Now you are My true Poor Clare, vowed to love and expiation. Root up the slightest feeling contrary to love. Henceforth do not lose a moment. Be on the watch to use every opportunity for offering Me an act of reparation. All that time is lost when you are occupied far from Me. Watch and pray." (No. 151).

Sister Mary of the Trinity also wrote the following on a piece of paper already containing Notes and dated July 1, 1941:

"+Jesus! Resolutions of retreat, December 8, 1941: Exactitude, schedule, rule,

harness my imagination
no more imposing myself,
no more boasting."

The fervor of her commitment was evident. One
of her Sisters gave this testimony regarding Sister
Mary of the Trinity: "She had a foreboding of her
death. She prepared for it. Ever since our annual
retreat, finished on December 8, 1941, several religious noticed a real transformation in her. She was
a subject of edification by her meditation and her
attentive charity." Sister Mary of the Trinity was
reproducing in her everyday living the requests
Jesus makes of His victim souls: ". . .to listen to Me
more than to speak to Me; to strive to reproduce
My actions—My way of acting rather than My
words. . .to confine their efforts to spreading My
Spirit, My gentleness, and My kindness which does
not dwell on evil, but overcomes evil by good. By
being exacting with no one but themselves, they will
help souls, by their silence and their respect, to receive the graces which their fidelity and their
sacrifices will obtain from God." (No. 366).

It had been on August 16, 1941, that Sister Mary
of the Trinity received the first announcement of
her approaching death, more than ten months before it would occur: "Put your affairs in order; hold
yourself ready because I shall soon come to fetch
you. I shall come to fetch you all of a sudden." (No.
26). Hereafter there are numerous references to her
death in the Notes, forming a beautiful program of
preparation for that crowning act of life.

Our Lord first gently manifested His prerogative
as Master of Life and Death by telling the Sister

early in the winter of that same year: "They give you more to eat. That is well. They will see more clearly when I come to fetch you that it is I who have come and that there is no other cause." (No. 36). "Do your duty faithfully and as perfectly as possible; alter nothing in your manner of living; neither penances nor mortifications will change the hour at which I shall come to fetch you." (No. 57).

However, if there were no exterior situations that would affect His coming, there was an interior reality which would have a profound bearing. "Prepare yourself. Do all that you have to do, and as much and as well as you can." (No. 36). "Prepare yourself—strip yourself—I want you to be wholly, wholly Mine." (No. 54). "I am impatient to have you all Mine. Prepare yourself. When you are ready, I will come and fetch you." (No. 67). "Rejoice, My Beloved! Are you not in a hurry to join Me?...I long to keep you near Me; I long for you to finish your preparation! Do penance in body and soul by greater vigilance in these days that remain—that your soul may be purified and that it may fly to Me when I call you." (No. 136)

At first Sister Mary of the Trinity questioned: "When will it be?" The reply was simple and brief: "When you are ready." (No. 145). Soon her question would be: "My Lord Jesus, what ought I do [to prepare]?" She received many instructions: "There must not be a single fiber in your being which escapes love. There must not be a single regret in your soul, a single resentment, a single feeling of bitterness, or of antipathy. Love all My creatures for My sake, love Me through them; and love things and circumstances as expressions of My action and My will. With the same intensity, hate and flee from My enemies; I have already named them once: lying, duplicity, noise—restlessness—disorder!...Establish *order* within yourself, and disorder, all by itself, will disappear within you and around you. It is sufficient to overcome evil by good." (No. 243).

Side by side with this lofty program were practical, everyday details: "Keep silence. Be a little more mortified at table. Let yourself each day be a little more stripped: of material things and of treasures of the heart and mind, so as to receive all from My hands." (No. 244). And always the recurring theme: "When you are ready, I will call you." (No. 244).

This thought of death would always be present to her. One day, one of the Sisters said to her: "Time on earth is long, on a journey, far from the Lord. I would be happy to die soon."

"No, not you, rather I," replied Sister Mary of the Trinity with verve. "I hope that the first grave to be dug will be for me!" Nevertheless, nothing at the time let one suspect a near end. It seems from Our Lord's reproach that at certain moments the Sister doubted this herself: "I shall soon come to fetch you, even though you do not believe it and are enjoying excellent health." (No. 145). This distrust was no doubt also the cause of the Lord's apparent delay in calling her: she was still not aware of the detailed preparation that He was asking of her, and that she had several months in which to work at it, with ever-increasing generosity and love.

Sister Mary of the Trinity, emboldened by the promise she had received on the day of her Vow of Victim—"henceforth your prayers will obtain conversions..."—never ceased to plead for that of her relatives. She was told: "Do not doubt the conversion of your relatives—I have My time, and My means are not your means. Do you really understand that if I enter into the lives, it is with the Cross that I enter into the lives and into the hearts of those who are Mine...?" (No. 253). The Sister's generous victim spirit could only reply: "Make them find You, You and Your Church, and grant that I may carry a little of their Cross, so that they may not be crushed by it." (No. 253). She thus showed how well she understood what "my heavenly Mother said to me" in the first and only written communication of the Holy Mother of God: "My life was a succession of trials more incomprehensible than yours. Nevertheless, I always loved. Love never left my heart. I knew that the salvation of souls is bought by the Blood of my Son and by our tears— yes, the tears of the heart..." (No. 341).

"Love never left my heart." The call of Christ had separated Louisa Jaques from all her relatives. To answer it, she had become Sister Mary of the Trinity in a Catholic convent in a far distant country. But the profound affection which united the members of this family surmounted the test.

Her relatives were present in all of Sister Mary's prayers. She never ceased asking for them the light which would lead them to share her happiness in the Church, to receive the same Sacraments. When Our Lord declared: "I also am all yours. What do you desire?" her response was immediate: "O my God, my God! You know! The conversion of my family. For them also: 'Your love and Your grace' and Your Sacraments..." (No. 547).

For their part, through regular correspondence, her family never stopped telling Sister Mary of their affection. Her father, who was then 77 years old, wrote to her for her birthday and for the big feasts of the year: "My dear Louisa . . ." and he ended: "Believe me, your affectionate father who loves you."

Her brothers and sisters, dispersed by the war, sent her news. Her two "little" brothers, mobilized in the Army of Egypt, had planned to visit her during a holiday; unfortunately, they could not obtain the necessary visas in time. Before there would be another opportunity, Sister Mary had left this earth.

In the beginning of the year 1942, Sister Mary wrote several letters which show how faithful she remained to her friendships and to what point she retained concern for the happiness of friends and relatives.

In January, Feast of the Holy Family, it was a message to Bluette:

"I am happy in my vocation, you know it, you perhaps guessed it. I would like to be able to say it in such a way that my happiness radiates so that it falls joyously into the souls of others. But I don't know how to talk, and the happiness of a Poor Clare is so interior that it cannot be explained very well. One guesses it. They say that one enters the pathway toward perfection; I believe that I am not yet there and I don't know if I will be there, but I notice that I have entered a pathway of amazement. There is nothing more beautiful than drawing closer to the Lord Jesus!"

The following Sunday, it was a long response to her sister Alice:

"What a joy, what a great joy, your letter of October 4! It arrived right at the end of the year as

if to announce a new year. Reassuring news on the
fate of my relatives. There was an awfully long time
(it seems to me) that I knew nothing of you. What
happiness to know that all of you are well!...

"Youth, oh! the picnics behind La Layette...what
memories full of sunshine and perfumed with the
sap of pine trees, molasses tarts, salted cookies, wild
strawberries...What a childhood! How we loved each
other and how life has scattered us...But love remains, it has deep roots, it will be stronger than
death...

"Oh! the memories! I have a golden harvest of
them, but the reaping is for later in the hours of
the big feast days and leisure activities. They remain in reserve like some Italian leathers kept for
you and the children. It seemed to me on reading
your letter that I saw 'Little Mother' and the drawer
of her chest, the drawer with the treasures. You did
well to keep back thus some surprises for them. That
develops in children the sense of respect for things,
not through avarice or economy, but because of the
beauty which is so fragile. It remains intact if we
don't touch it. The sense of delicacy, of respect, is
innate, one has it or one does not have it...

"Good-bye, my beloved sister. Pray for me, too. It
is there that we find each other in the Heart of God
who awaits us...

Your Sister Mary of the Trinity."

The affectionate, loving heart of Sister Mary of
the Trinity, refined in the crucible of the love of God
and taught unceasingly by Him, manifested a selfless concern and tender care for her Sisters and Superiors. This became very evident on the Reverend

Mother Abbess's feast day, celebrated on one of the first days of February. Her Sisters testified: "Each year at the time of this feast day, the young professed religious was not the same as in ordinary times. Dominating her timidity and her reserve, she ingeniously set about to stimulate the activity of each of her Sisters so that the feast day might be a success and that Reverend Mother might be happy. She composed or asked one of her Sisters to compose a recital, some songs; she painted or sketched with originality."

This thoughtfulness and generosity, always characteristic of the Sister, was encouraged by Jesus in details of homely practicality: "You must finish your Sisters' work before your own. If your little things are not ready for Reverend Mother's feast, it does not matter. I will see to it—but watch that your Sisters' things are finished and that all are happy." (No. 277). But it was also tempered, and always her vision was directed to the essential: "Do not get excited over a feast that only lasts for a day. What is it? I am inviting you to a Feast for all Eternity. Stay near Me." (No. 278).

Other testimony from her Sisters illustrates well her attitude toward her Superiors: ". . . she had more frequent contacts with the Reverend Mother, showing her the most affectionate respect, trying to find out what could cause her the greatest joy. . .

"The Reverend Mother did not want to have the necessary water brought up to her cell by others, insisting on serving herself. Sister Mary of the Trinity arranged things so well that she was successful in rendering this slight service each day." The respect and courtesy in the presence of authority

natural to the Sister was encouraged by the Lord:
"Love, love your Sisters. Love your Superiors much;
they have need of it. But in silence." (No. 42). "In
the same way as you try to please your Spouse, strive
to please your Superiors; anticipate their desires;
do what they like, that they may feel themselves
loved by you, loved in a special way." (No. 10). After
the death of Sister Mary of the Trinity, knowing
absolutely nothing about her interior communications, her Abbess on June 30, 1942, witnessed spontaneously to the faithfulness of the Sister to these
teachings: "What a beautiful little soul! No one else
showed me such attention and tenderness."

In order that this love should be shielded from
being a mere human feeling and attachment, the
Sister was instructed further on the role of authority
as seen with the vision of faith. "Love your Superiors
in the spirit of faith; you are united to Me when
you are united to them." (No. 534). "My little daughter, I wish you daily to offer a special prayer to My
Mother for Superiors, all Superiors...Authority is
sacred; it comes from God. It should be a protection
for those confided to it, imitating in their regard
My Mother's way of acting...making the same demands as God makes, and being itself a source of
grace for its children. Authority should reveal to its
subjects something of the goodness of the Father,
and of the demands of the God of Holiness—
something of the obedience of the Son—something
of the boundless generosity and the wisdom of the
Holy Spirit...Its mission is to lead souls to God.
Pray each day, at every Communion, for Superiors."
(No. 446).

"Human love is fragile. It requires much respect.

You must *accept* it and obey its inspirations." (No. 580). Because of this fragility of love, the relationships Sister Mary of the Trinity formed with her Sisters were frequently the subject of communications from Our Lord. On January 1, 1941, He said: "Be kind to *all* your Sisters and Superiors. Judge no one." (No. 17). Shortly thereafter: "Love does not see injuries. It always forgives without growing weary; it loves unceasingly and is ever growing." (No. 22). "Strive to be gentle." (No. 241). Because of the tendency of the Sister to demand much of herself and of others, He gently warned her: "You will never regret having been mistaken in judging a person to be better than she is, because you must see in others what they are capable of becoming with My grace, and not stamp them according to what they are at that time." (No. 389). "Show confidence in your Sisters; you must believe in their good intentions." (No. 265).

This human love was not to remain at the human level. It was to rise through sacrifices and detachment, based on love of God. One of the lessons Jesus taught her was to love disinterestedly: ". . . love without asking for anything in return; and wait patiently until you too are loved. Never refuse to give pleasure." (No. 66). The pleasure one should give is never that which is contrary to the other's spiritual good: "This is love; to clothe others with that which shall make them pleasing to God. To give them even our ideas, the best of our thoughts. . . Not merely to tolerate their appropriation of them but to *adorn* them with all that can make them beautiful." (No. 116). And again: "You must love your Sisters from the bottom of your heart, spontaneously—not by an act of will. Love them as you love Me, because it is I whom you love in them. Love them because they need it to become better." (No. 525).

From the comments already quoted of her Sisters and Superiors, it is clear that Sister Mary of the Trinity was generous in her response to these invitations to purify and expand her love of others. The spiritual dimension of friendship had always been important to her. Now, as she prepared for the final profession of vows which she would not live long enough to make, she turned to Bluette, desiring to strengthen the union of their souls by a new relationship in the Spirit.

On February 8, Sexagesima Sunday, Sister Mary of the Trinity began a letter for Bluette. Very busy during these days, she did not finish it before the 20th of the same month:

". . . I would have a lot to tell you, so much that I don't know where to begin. Although there are no extraordinary events in our so carefully regulated life, there are, however, many little things which make it interesting in what they reveal about solicitude, about forethought on the part of God. I am quite astonished to see that here, too, one year does not resemble the preceding one even though there are the same feasts, the same liturgy, the same ceremonies, the same work in the monastery. One has other preoccupations, other immediate interests and other joys. During the three and one half years that I have been here, we have lost, each year, one of our Sisters. It is the oldest ones who are calling each other into Paradise. But the novitiate does not get filled up with the same rhythm as the cemetery.

"(February 20) This letter is coming apart at the

seams! We cannot write except on Sunday or in moments during the day which may be available.

"Thus I profit from the chance to come running to you before Lent leads us into the great silence. What will this Lent be like? I always fear it, I do not know why, although meditation on the Passion, is, I believe, the only subject of meditation to which my mind goes spontaneously, almost constantly. Oh, to understand, to understand! One retains the words on the lips and the gestures of what is said to God, but interior comprehension, oh, what a revelation and what a change it produces in our poor soul...You have already drawn down on me many special graces, I am convinced of it. That is why I would like, in spite of the war and exterior difficulties of corresponding which could oppose it, for you to be my 'Godmother of Profession,' if that pleases you. We all choose a 'Godmother of Profession' even if she is far away. That signifies a protection and a spiritual collaboration which consolidates this union of souls of the same faith, of goodwill, that Our Lord wants so much. 'Let them all be *one*.' It is thus that I understand this office of Godmother of Profession. No need to send a beautiful present—for me, that is very secondary—but to assume a union of efforts and of prayer. Do you want to?..."

On February 13 of that year, the Sister wrote the first lines of the account of her conversion and vocation. It had been 16 years since "this insignificant incident happened to me. It was wordless, it was like a dream, and yet it was real—and it changed my whole life." Perhaps in response to the Sister's question, "Why that mysterious event?" she was told: "Yes, I wished to draw you to Myself. You are on the right path. Continue on it. Do not waste your time in bothering about what others are doing. *'Follow thou Me.'* " (No. 296).

Ash Wednesday fell on February 18. The Sister placed this Lent under the protection and guidance of Mary, Mediatrix of all Graces. "Teach me to live this Lent as Jesus desires—this Lent may be the last in this poor life..." It was in fact to be so. Was it in response to this prayer that she was told: "For a soul to give Me pleasure, it must have at least one trait that resembles My Mother: at least one trait...Then since I have so much joy in contemplating something which is like My Mother, I forget the rest, I see only that...Thus My Mother covers you with a coat." (Unpublished Note).

A Note found on a calendar page and dated February 26 says: "You complain? but you don't take a step without My holding you up. But you are completely Mine, you belong to Me, you are Mine." After a few lines crossed out the Note continues: "Recall My entire life, the washing of the feet, My Passion...And if sometimes I wanted you to associate yourself with My humiliations! Be thankful!"

Other previously unpublished Notes, discovered on the back of a letter, seem to belong to this same period:

"You must give Me what I want, not what you want to offer Me...If you want to give Me pleasure, do exactly what your Father ordered you to do.

"Being on time at Office, even a few minutes early, and with the rules, since it is to Me that you come.

"Silence.

"Gentleness, gentleness, gentleness with all.

"I need you to give Me these three things."

"When obedience is the action of love it makes reparation for everything.

"The act of obedience makes reparation for revolts of nature.

"The act of interior obedience which nobody will ever know consoles Me for the forgetfulness of My creatures.

"The misunderstood act of obedience, which perhaps will draw reproaches or disdain from men, consoles Me for the scorn that My creatures make of the life of the Man of Sorrows.

"Yes, that is what consoles Me."

It was also during this Lenten period that the Sister was told: "My little daughter, you have much to learn and to put into practice: each day learn one little thing, one thing at a time which you will henceforth practice; each day one thing and I shall be pleased." (No. 368). Was it putting that advice into action that prompted her to note on a piece of letter paper a byword for each day from March 9 to March 22?

+Jesus! Experience

March 9 You should aim above all at harmony, at a union among you. In secondary matters that can be rectified, it is better to put up with them patiently than try to seek improvements if that harms the amiability of our dealings with each other.

In *secondary* matters.

March 10 There is a real spiritual gain and joy in choosing the least rather than the best for one's advantage.

March 11 It is one of the privileges of cloistered life: I can be sure that they will criticize me and they will speak ill of me. To act and exist solely for the Lord Jesus. To be before my neighbor as before God.

March 12 'It is not what you give which gives pleasure to her who receives it and to Me, it is the amiability with which one must give.'

March 13 A day of work almost without interior dialogue, a day almost lost.

March 14 The fewer words there are, the stronger the thought is. The suavity of the words erases the thought.

I must practice being silent. *Urgent*.

March 15 Work: rather do less, but be ready before the time indicated, that is the secret of giving pleasure.

March 16 When I make a mistake in work, I must not hide it, rather explain.

March 17 *Prudence* in letters; no allusions which can be misinterpreted.

March 18 Surmount evil with good, suspicions with confidence.

March 19 Entertain *hope,* like a tabernacle light in our soul.

March 20 Do not hide anything, except in rare, absolute necessity.

March 21 Order: don't leave our papers lying around.

March 22 Regularity in keeping the great silence whatever the cost."

On March 18, Sister Mary of the Trinity celebrated
the anniversary of her Baptism. The next day, the
Feast of Saint Joseph, she noted this communication: "Yes, it is 14 years ago that I drew you to Myself. Baptism, First Communion. I waited long for
you. What have I not given you?...You are My beloved little child; I redeemed you by My Passion...If
you obey My voice, that is a great good; I will do
the rest. Is it not I who have done everything in
your life?" (No. 385). Evidently much moved by this
remembrance of the Lord's work in her life, the Sister wrote on a page in her Notebook everything of
which this date reminded her:

19 March 1928 Milan	Baptism Communion
19 March 1929 Bergamo	Countess Agliardi
19 March 1930 Milan	Postulant Missionary
	Sisters of Egypt
19 March 1931	
La Chaux-de-Fonds	Postulant Society
19 March 1932 id.	Novice Society
19 March 1933 id.	id. Society
19 March 1934 Neuchâtel	id. Society
19 March 1935 Reims	Professed Society
19 March 1936 Neuchâtel	id. Society
19 March 1937 Evian	Postulant Poor Clare
19 March 1938 Johannesburg	Family
19 March 1939 Jerusalem	Postulant Poor Clare
19 March 1940 id.	Novice
19 March 1941 id.	

The Sister did not record the present date, March
19, 1942, when she had attained the goal of being
"My true Poor Clare" (No. 151), a professed Sister

in Jerusalem. Did she on this day suspect that when she would again celebrate Saint Joseph's Feast, the place would be the Heavenly Jerusalem? It is probable, as the Note already alluded to continues with several references to her death. "Why do you fear to come to Me?. . .Death will lead you to your God; and I am always with you. . .What do you fear? Prepare yourself." (No. 385).

Spiritual writers in every age have been careful to indicate the damage the soul sustains by attachments, no matter how small. Saint John of the Cross uses the comparison of a captive bird. What does it matter if it is held fast by a silken thread or a stout rope? It cannot fly. Saint Colette of Corbie, to whom reference has already been made, warns her Sisters in her Testament to "hold all the rest suspect, such as books, chaplets, thread, needles. . .to which your special affection might cling." During this last Lent of Sister Mary of the Trinity, the Notes report to us in a touching and very instructive way one of the final interior struggles of the Sister and show the importance of "little things" as occasions of love or refusal. The demands of the inner Voice, the reason for these requests in the Sister's life as well as the role of natural joys as invitations to higher happiness, the importance of selfless sharing—in a word, our human situation seen from the vantage point of Eternity—all is richly woven together, or should we say, stitched together by the Divine Artist in this episode of the lace!

Sister Mary of the Trinity knew many embroidery stitches, and she had her little collection of patterns, pictures clipped from magazines. Her Superiors had recourse to her artistic talents for the more delicate work. To show the thanks of the community to a family of benefactors, the Superior had just accepted an order for a little piece of luxury work: a tablecloth.

Sister Mary worked on it with the other Sisters. On April 12, the inner Voice intervened for the first time. "Be kind! Give way to your Sisters' wishes. Teach them how to make that lace, since they have such a longing to learn." Immediately He stated the motive from the Sister's own life: "You have other joys. . ." (No. 448). And then in the lives of her Sisters: "You hinder the flowering of My life in your Sisters' souls when you cause them some displeasure or vexation: yes, it is I who suffer through it." (No. 449). The very next day the communication took the form of a rebuke, gentle but with a touch of irony. "My little daughter, who would believe that you would pay more attention to a piece of common embroidery than to your Lord!. . .You think too much about your lace and you neglect Me. Who would believe it. . .?" (No. 455). " 'If your eye is for you an occasion of falling, pluck it out. . .' Be quick in finishing that lace that fascinates you too much: is it not My Voice alone that must captivate you?. . ." (No. 456). On April 15, a spiritual exchange was proposed to the Sister, and again the work for which she was destined was placed before her. "Give Me your lace by letting your Sisters do it. And I will give you more beautiful embroidery to do in souls." (No. 459).

As the inner struggle continued, the exterior work was taking shape under the skillful fingers of Sister Mary of the Trinity working together with her Sisters. While all were eager for instruction, one among them, a young Sister of Armenian origin with extremely nimble fingers, was very desirous of learning. "Oh! Show me how you do it," she often asked Sister Mary of the Trinity. With her natural ability, she quickly learned the new stitches and even surpassed her teacher in their execution.

Sister Mary was mortified by it! For several days she refused to share her knowledge and concealed her "patterns." The struggle within the Sister is thus revealed: "You who promised to teach your little Sisters a certain embroidery *later on* are scandalized because they do not believe you and are trying to find out at once how you do it . . ." From this experience with her own state of soul a lesson was drawn: "Do you not believe that I am as sensitive to lack of confidence as you are? I have promised you the grace of certain conversions—because they have not already taken place, do you doubt My Word . . . ?" (No. 460).

As the interior trial persisted, the place of such good and desirable human enjoyments was pointed out. Thus the Lord did not condemn the work as such but only the attachment to it, the trace of selfishness displayed in the temporary refusal to share knowledge and skills. "It is because you all need some human natural joys to encourage you toward the generosity that will reveal supernatural joys to you, that I want you to give the lace to your little Sisters, as they have such a great longing for it. You have something else to do and I give you other joys." (No. 464). "You are not kind enough. Be kinder and more generous with your little Sisters. Give in to their wishes. Even if you gave them all that you use for doing your little tasks and the little pictures

which distract you, what would you lose?...There is
a time to find joy in little material tasks...there is
a time to find one's joy in the communications of the
Spirit; enter into that phase—and make the others
happy. I desire that all those around you should be
happy: you can contribute to that..." (No. 477).

There is yet another aspect which must not be
overlooked. Sister Mary of the Trinity's skill in the
work, her pleasure and enjoyment in executing it
must have been evident to her Sisters. In relinquish-
ing all this in favor of her Sisters, they, and all who
would subsequently learn of this episode, would draw
a significant lesson from it. "I desire that your
detachment from material things may make people
understand that there are other values to which
one's time, one's care and one's affection must be
given..." (No. 478).

A week after the little inner drama had begun,
the Sister was told quite bluntly: "Get rid of your
pictures, as your Father told you—you will not be
bored. I will never abandon you. I have things to
say to you." (No. 479). The next day again: "Listen
to Me and write. Do not do any more embroidery,
unless your Superior asks it of you." (No. 486). That
the battle was not yet over is revealed in the re-
bukes of the two following communications: "At last
you are giving away your lace. Why did you not do
it sooner? During all this time I have still had to
wait for you...See the disturbance that your selfishness has caused in the souls that were in need
of your generosity..." (No. 487). "You have disappointed Me. If you had been detached from your embroidery and all that distracts you from Me, as I
asked you, you would have had the strength to be

more generous; disagreements and sins of envy would not have crept in among you; see how responsible you are." (No. 488). Finally winning a victory over herself, she gave everything to her Sisters. But the battle had lasted about 10 days.

After following with sympathetic understanding born of our common humanness the successful completion of this inner trial, perhaps we should look to the opposite conclusion to make more explicit the parallel to our own situation. Each new grace depends largely upon fidelity to the present grace. So the question could even be posed: What if Sister Mary of the Trinity had not been faithful in this one instance, this seemingly small circumstance? It cannot be determined actually but one wonders, would the communications have continued? Would the conversion and vocation account have been written? Would the Message have been given to us? Certainly the answers are hidden from us and such questions are futile except to highlight individual responsibility to whatever grace is asking.

Already on April 16, Sister Mary of the Trinity had been told: "It is I who gave you your vocation, and the desire for your vocation, and the means to realize it. See, see how I have waited for you...how I have traced out your path...You may write the story of your vocation briefly, for your Father...it will interest him to see in detail one of the manifold manifestations of My love—you will do it to *thank* Me, My little daughter..." (No. 476). "Write in short sentences. Try to put down all that concerns your vocation, even the details. Omit the rest." (No. 505). "Write the story of your vocation quickly, without delay and without lingering over it—I have other more important messages to give you afterward." (No. 510). An urgency is sensed in these encouragements to write quickly. Although the Sister did not realize it, she had scarcely two months left to receive and record the "more important messages." Because of her faithfulness to Love's demands, the Sister could continue her close union with the Lord. She was ready for the task for which she had been freed. "Now you are rid of the embroidery! Henceforth I wish you to keep your free moments for Me." (No. 511). It was on this day, May 1, that the Sister began the account of her conversion and vocation, ". . .the story of your cowardice, and the story of My mercy." (No. 563).

During this writing, the purpose of this work was a matter of some concern to the Sister. She wondered, "Why?" The answer received was enigmatic: "You ask Me why I have told you to write the account of your poor vocation—it does not matter much to you. I am content that you should do it. Finish it quickly; arrange to give it to your Father, then think no more about it. It is done, it is of no further importance to you." (No. 552). The work was probably concluded shortly after this communication of May 12, certainly before May 23. We learn on this later date of the desire of the Sister to destroy the account. This time the "Why?" is from Jesus: "Why do you want to burn the account of your vocation?. . .What does it matter to you, since you have written it for Me?" (No. 590). Always the eyes of the Sister were directed away from herself, toward her Lord.

If faithfulness to grace prepares the heart for fresh

graces, we may wonder how much strength Sister Mary of the Trinity derived from her obedience to the request to write the story of her vocation and from the seemingly small conflict over the lace to arm her for the far more difficult and serious trial before her.

The very discreet reference to temptations against her vocation which began early in January have already been alluded to: "If you remain here. . ." On February 17, she had been cautioned: "Walk as if holding Me by the hand. You have dark hours to pass through, but I will be with you, as if holding you by the hand." (No. 307). A few months before her death, Sister Mary of the Trinity underwent a painful purification by test, misunderstanding, the feeling of an insurmountable incomprehension.

These somber hours were the last, but the most painful, of a long interior struggle. Her confessor adds: "These words are a very discreet revelation, since in fact these temptations, even by their level calmness, were more terrible because less perceptible than if they had been manifested by a great interior upheaval. In appearance, in her work, in her relationships with her neighbor, it was serenity, the same attentive fidelity. At the very bottom of her soul, it was a drama which she did not seem to realize herself."

God alone was able to measure its danger. The confessor remembered clearly. . . She herself did not see the danger which was threatening her, nor the devil's trap. Besides, he had taken good care to camouflage his hand under the attractive exterior of a greater perfection.

For three weeks at least, she had begged the

confessor to help her leave, to enter another order.

At the origin of this temptation, a misunderstanding with the Superiors, for which she was not in the least guilty, produced in her an insurmountable disgust for her life. An incident, which could have been repeated and for which she was not responsible, escaped from her "to save appearances." She let herself be surprised and her emotion prevented her from realizing from the start the gravity of her way of acting. But the strictness of her conscience provoked a reaction which threw her at the feet of the Master. She received the following light on the matter: "My daughter, the Truth of My teaching abolishes all compromise. It forbids duplicity, deception toward your Superiors or inferiors. It is not enough to know My teaching; I ask you to live it...do not allow yourself a *single* compromise, a single deceit. Rather exaggerate your integrity toward your Superiors and your Sisters—that I may always find you sincere and true." (No. 306).

She went through other trials; this one was the hardest and longest.

Under the influence of grace, peace was established in her soul. As often happens with profound natures and with people who have suffered deeply, she did not possess a natural gaiety. But she learned to receive trials peaceably, to keep them for herself, and to give to others only gentleness and joy. A smile almost always lit up her face. When, after her death, the confessor requested a photograph of her as a religious from the Poor Clares of Jerusalem, the reply received is revealing: "We have a small identity card photograph of her, that is all. It is certainly like her, but we do not find in it either the animation of her eyes or the sweetness of her smile. Only those who lived with her knew the expression on the face of that Sister. . . her living face will remain well hidden."

Was it in the calm following the prolonged tempest that the Sister realized the import of this truth: "When your soul is in peace, you think that I am pleased with you—when it is agitated by great storms, do not think that I am not pleased with you—you do not *feel* it, but it is in those moments that I come to your help and draw you nearer to Me." (No. 600).

To be drawn nearer to Jesus; for Sister Mary of the Trinity that was to share His sufferings. She had been told: "I have brought you to Jerusalem that together we may ascend Calvary." (No. 65). This thought must have been often in her meditation. On May 18, while praying in the convent garden from where can be seen the Mount of Olives and Mount Sion, the Sister was reminded that ". . . here in these places I suffered and consummated My Passion. Here I was laughed at by all, mocked, scoffed, betrayed. . . here that I gave all My Blood. . . *I*, your God, the Son of God. Do you understand what you have to do if you love Me? Do you understand what this means: 'to follow Me'. . .?" (No. 571).

The earnestness of Sister Mary of the Trinity in striving to "love Me. . . to follow Me. . ." found a singular expression in two notes written and signed with her blood. The first of these is dated October 28, 1939, two months after she had been clothed with the cross-form habit of Saint Clare:

"+Jesus!

"I, Sister Mary of the Trinity, offer to my Saviour Jesus the promise to obey *blindly* everything that obedience can ask me while imploring His aid.

"Jerusalem   Saint Clare"

The second prayer, which is undated, has already been quoted in comparison with a prayer of Saint Colette:

"+Jesus!

"I abandon myself for health, for sickness, for life, for death, in all my desires, in all my conduct, to work henceforth only for Your glory, the return of Protestants to the Church. There is nothing henceforth that I do not want to undertake for love of You.

"Saint Colette, our Mother, help me!

"Our mother Saint Clare.

"Our mother Saint Colette, pray for me! Amen."

Jesus expressed His approval of this rather unusual gesture in a communication of May 24. "Yes, there are certain prayers that must be signed with one's own blood. . ." (No. 599). On this Pentecost Sunday, the Sister was also reminded of her approaching death. "That a holocaust may be complete, the destruction of the victim is necessary." (No. 596). Granting the possibility that the Sister wrote other prayers with her blood which have not been preserved, it is at least a plausible hypothesis to assign this second prayer before this date.

It must be cautioned that if the words noted above approved this gesture, it was because these prayers were signed first by fidelity to duty. It is in this exact obedience that a religious soul "sheds her blood" every day for Christ.

As the month of June opened, the canonical visitation of the Jerusalem Monastery took place. According to Church law, the Bishop of the area that a monastery depends on, or his delegate, receives each Sister individually; he gathers information on the way in which they observe the Rule and on the quality of community life; he listens to the observations or suggestions of each. Reference to such a canonical visitation was made in the section on Sister Mary of the Trinity's postulancy with the Poor Clares of Evian. Was the experience of the Sister in that particular situation the reason for the abundant communications of these days with their calls to confidence, abandonment in the hands of God, sincerity?

From this time on the Notes refer primarily to the canonical visitation, always a time of trial and of grace. Within them much illumination is shed on the mystery of the religious life, especially the cloistered religious life. It is called a mystery, for the worth of such a life belongs to the realm of faith.

The following communication gives an example of this faith response. It is addressed to all religious rather than just the Sister. "Your life is very great. My little daughter, the least act of obedience, because it is done in union with Me, the least fidelity to your Holy Rule, has its repercussion on the entire Church. Would you believe it? In the same way your failings, the smallest of your acts of cowardice, has its repercussion on the entire world—by its consequences—would you believe it?" (No. 643). The double "Would you believe it?" reveals the struggle necessary for religious themselves to keep the dignity and value of their living before their gaze. This value and dignity is defined by the Church and safeguarded by the Church. Hence this communication, addressed again to all: "My little daughter, your time, your Holy Rule, your vows no longer belong to you. I gave them to you because you wished to consecrate them to Me. You have no right to live them according to your fancy; you must live them according to the spirit of the Church. The Church is I...The convent does not belong to you—it is loaned to you. You have no right to live there according to your own ideas— you must live there as the Church directs. Because the Church is I." (Nos. 652, 653).

Perhaps the most moving and telling communication is this simple injunction: "Say: 'It is such a great privilege to have a vocation to the religious life that to safeguard it one shuts one's eyes to everything.' " (No. 638).

What bothers one today did not do so yesterday. It will not do so tomorrow. Why? Changing dispositions, moods. Or it may be a more serious situation that cannot be altered, so one concentrates upon acceptance rather than the unavoidable. All, every person, may derive spiritual consolation and profit by remembering the great privilege it is to be a religious, to be a Christian, to belong to Jesus! This emphasis on the essential in life neither disregards nor disdains other elements of natural and supernatural existence. Simply focusing on the right place gives proper perspective to all else.

As the visitation closed, the same requests were once again reiterated to the Sister "...do not separate yourself from My meekness...overcome evil by good...console Me by being more faithful." (No. 656, 662).

NOTES

1. This and subsequent "Notes" are from *The Spiritual Legacy of Sister Mary of the Holy Trinity* (reprint edition, TAN Books and Publishers, Inc., 1981).
2. In speaking to Sister Mary of the Trinity in French, Our Lord used the second person singular (*tu*) when His words were especially for her own personal guidance, even though they might also be helpful to others. When He used the second person plural (*vous*), however, His words were meant for her entire community or for all religious or even for all Christians. In order to maintain this significant distinction in the English translation, the words "you" and "your" have been underlined in all passages in which the French text has the plural form *vous*.

4

LAST DAYS
(1942)

Toward the middle of June, a new return of the flu put the whole community in a piteous state of health. Sister Mary of the Trinity seemed to escape the epidemic, but in fact, she was more gravely sick and had been already for several days. On June 8 or 9 she had been forewarned: "It will be soon." (No. 659). She had the promise of her Lord: "As a proof [that it is He who speaks to her] you will have the strength that I will give you to bear with patience and love the sufferings that will come to you." (No. 585). With this grace and her great energy she was able to hide her suffering, but they caught her leaning on the wall to go fulfill her work in the refectory. As soon as she heard someone coming, she would stand up straight, trying to smile.

On June 16, seeing her so tired, a Sister offered to help her in her work. She thanked her with much affection, saying to her: "I want to do my little duty right up to the end." The next day, she still accompanied on the harmonium the chant of Benediction of the Blessed Sacrament after Mass. In the morning, Reverend Mother took her to the infirmary; she had more than 104°F fever. The infirmarian and several Sisters understood that all hope of saving her was lost. Sister Mary of the Trinity knew this better than anyone else, for on this day when she was confined to bed she was asked for her final surrender: "I can cure you whenever I wish, if I wish—but I have called you—will you come?" (No. 665). Her *fiat* was prompt and wholehearted: "Yes, my Lord Jesus, yes."

Summoned immediately, the doctor diagnosed typhoid fever. Was it a brusque reawakening of the illness which had menaced her so often? The illness seemed to affect especially her lungs. She said her chest was on fire. But right up to the end, not a single complaint escaped her lips.

The confessor of the community, Father Silvère, came to see her several times. On June 20, she felt so weak that she thought the moment of departure had arrived; she then gave him the story of her conversion and the piece of paper where she related the apparition of February 13, 1926, without adding a single word of explanation.

This final purification through the suffering of illness was to last five more days.

She could not take any nourishment and, in spite of her fever, scarcely anything to drink. Her weakness became so great that she could not even hold the glass to sip water. Besides this, the temperature during those days was stifling, as one rarely sees in Jerusalem.

The poor patient talked about the "fresh air of the mountains of Switzerland." On June 23, two days before her death, she still scribbled this with a pencil:

"How good God is, good, good, good! I feel like crying when I think about it. He lets me think I am on vacation in Switzerland, in the country of

fresh mountain air, as we have twice been able to
meet there with my sister from America [her beloved Alice]. This morning after Holy Communion,
He conducted me to each of those places we crossed
and He showed me souls, many souls that He is calling, that He waits for. He showed me many of them
and in the most diverse milieus:

'Do you see, My little daughter, they would like
to give themselves to Me, but they cannot enter the
religious life, so what to do?

'I want souls to know that by the Vow of Victim,
they enter a life of union with Me.

'They must know what the Vow of Victim signifies: *to imitate My Eucharistic Life.*

'I want there to be some of them everywhere, in
all situations.

'You will offer Me much, because of your Vow of
Victim, and by your Vow of Victim, so that souls
will understand the urgency.

'I want very much, wherever there are generous
souls, this Vow of Victim.

'You will suffer much, but I will be with you, and
I will come to fetch you all of a sudden.' " (No. 666).

These were the very last words the Sister was to
record.

She manifested no fear at the nearness of death.
She had known already in her life the experience
of being near death's door. This peace was rather
the fruit of her hard won confidence in the promises
that had been accorded her. "You must not fear
death; do you not know that I will be with you...?"
(No. 87). "Do you think I will abandon you at the
moment of death..?" (No. 145). "It is at the hour
of death that you will understand how much I have

loved you." (No. 174). She knew in whom she believed.

Feeling death approach, she did not neglect a single act of thoughtfulness: she begged Reverend Mother to write letters which she dictated to her, to all her close relatives. She asked if the Masses which were to be applied to her after her death could not be said rather for the return of Protestants to Unity. This desire was granted, but the Mother Abbess also had the Masses offered for the dead Sister.

She showed herself to be very thankful toward her nurses, trying to smile to the Sisters who came to visit her. Always courageous and spontaneous, the sick one responded to a Sister who was compassionating her: "But you don't have any energy!" To another sick religious, her neighbor, she sent a spiritual bouquet every evening by way of the Sister infirmarian—which the latter forgot on the way, contenting herself with saying, "They are very celestial and spiritual words for you. Nothing about health, nothing about earth, but it is too long and too beautiful for me to retain it!"

June 25, in the morning, the night having been very bad, they urgently called the Father confessor to come to the deathbed. She asked to go to confession. Then at 10:30, in the presence of the whole community, she received Extreme Unction. A few Sisters remained beside her. One of them comforted her by asking: "Are you indeed uniting your sufferings to those of Our Lord on the Cross?" She replied: "Oh! yes, with all my heart! I am happy to suffer; I would not want to suffer less." She murmured the invocation: "Saint Therese of the Child Jesus, pray for us." The story of the death of Saint

Therese, read about a month before, had greatly impressed her. At that time she was asked by Our Lord: "Would you want to suffer less?" (No. 554). Her response had been generous: "My God, You know all: my desire to expiate, to make reparation, to love You, to glorify You by suffering. . ." Then she added a sentence which reveals something of the manner and intimacy of these communications: "You are silent, my God, but I feel in Your silence that You accept it and that You will fulfill it. . .?" The fulfillment was taking place on this June day.

After the community meal, the Sisters of the "choir" came to sing for her a few verses of the song "Heaven in the Soul," a poem by Sister Elizabeth of the Trinity (Carmelite of Dijon). She thanked them, adding: "You must sing it again in the choir."

Toward 2:30 p.m. the Sisters present recited the Prayers for the Dying. She looked at them, one after the other, her face bathed in sweat. She asked: "I would like to drink." Then a little later: "I would like to sit up, to get up." Two Sisters helped her with caution; her gaze stopped on the picture of the Sacred Heart on the wall opposite the bed. . .("It is My Heart that awaits you."). . .Without anyone noticing it, her soul had flown away. The nurse put a little mirror in front of her mouth; it was finished, no breath came to cloud it. Quiet, calm, unperceived was His coming as He had foretold: "As a mother embraces her newborn child, so will I enfold you in My love." (No. 145).

"I will come to fetch you all of a sudden!" Sister Mary of the Trinity was with her Lord, with that Jesus whom she had so courageously sought, so ardently loved.

Her body lay in state in the choir. Her look was imposing, her eyes remained wide open. She seemed alive. All those who saw her through the grille were impressed.

Before revealing anything about the Notebooks, the confessor had asked the Reverend Mother to request the Sisters to communicate, in writing, what they might have noticed that was reprehensible in Sister Mary of the Trinity. The Superior excused herself from doing so for fear of scandalizing certain religious and provoking discussions which would be prejudicial in the community. Preoccupied nevertheless by this request, she risked a few days later asking an elderly Sister with a very deep prayer life. This Sister replied, "In my opinion, Sister Mary of the Trinity was a very gentle soul, very meditative. I would not be surprised if she had sometimes heard an interior voice."

It is a characteristic of life in the cloister that it be a hidden, unknown life and therefore apparently useless. The life of Sister Mary of the Trinity was not only hidden from the world; it was hidden from her own Sisters: not her exterior life—that did not escape observation—but nobody guessed at her interior life.

One of her former Superiors wrote that she had remained misunderstood. Rather, she passed unnoticed, unimportant to the others, exact in following the regulations of the house, faithful in accomplishing the work imposed on her; nothing had made her particularly noticed. It was part of God's plan for her: "You are My little Spouse: I will make your life more like My own...you are already united to Me at every moment—no one knows it, I wish it to be so—it is enough that your Sisters perceive My kindness through you." (No. 572). She was a soul who had been faithful in the way the Lord wished: "I wish them to be able to say at your death: 'She was a saint; she did very well all that she did.' That perfection in the common life is the sanctity that I ask of you. Nothing more." (No. 595).

When the secret of her intimacy with the Lord was finally revealed, a joyous astonishment spread through the monastery—all the more joyous because almost everyone seemed to say to herself: "I certainly was fooled by Sister Mary of the Trinity! She appeared to be nothing, one did not notice her and lo and behold...she was a privileged soul."

The explanation of this phenomenon is so obvious that it may pass unobserved. What passes more unnoticed, what appears to be more a mere nothing, what "fools" the senses more than the Eucharist, the Real Presence of Jesus hidden beneath the veil of bread? Jesus expressed it in this manner to the Sister: "I love to give Myself in Holy Communion...You see, to be better able to work in you, I make Myself small, so small, insignificant...So as to be able to communicate My Spirit better to those around you, would you be willing to make yourself small, quite small in your outward life, a mere nothing of no consequence, just an insignificant nonentity?" (No. 490). This was the way of living which was asked of Sister Mary of the Trinity. "What I ask of you, what I expect of you, is that you act...according to My way of acting, by imitating My Eucharistic Life...I have made Myself imitable in My human life—I have perpetuated My work

Louisa aged 10 months with her "Little Mother," Aunt Alice (Bornand), before their departure from Pretoria (1902).

The three sisters: Elizabeth, Alice, and Louisa (5 years old)—"an alert little girl with a determined look."

At L'Auberson in 1923, already 22 years old. What road shall she take?

Louisa before her departure for Italy (1926).

With Alice in the garden of Béthanie (1925).

August 1927: Vacation in the Valley of Binn (Canton of Valais).

Binn, 1927: Return from an excursion. From left to right: Thérèse Juvet, Véréna Pfenninger, Louisa, Bluette de Blaireville.

After Louisa's conversion. Her friend Bluette came to meet her in Milan to prepare with her for her entrance into the Church (June 1928). Bluette took back with her this photo from an afternoon walk with Louisa.

In the old house at L'Auberson (summer, 1930). On vacation with her parents. At left, Louisa's father.

On a walk at La Ferrière (Bernese Jura) with her friends. From left to right: Louisa, Véréna, Bluette. At this time Louisa was at La Chaux-de-Fonds (1931).

At La Chaux-de-Fonds (1932) with her friend Bluette.

Louisa when she was teaching in the Catholic school in Neuchâtel, after returning from Reims (fall, 1935).

In the harbor: Poor Clare at Jerusalem (1940). Her passport picture.

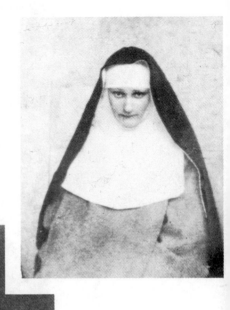

Cell of Sister Mary of the Trinity in the convent in Jerusalem.

The Jaques family gathered in Pretoria (1938). Standing, from left to right: Louisa, her half brother, Alice, Alexander, Elizabeth. Seated: the parents, Numa Jaques and his wife, stepmother of Louisa. In front: the children of Elizabeth and Alice.

+

O Père, qui êtes Dieu voici que je tends la main
pr. accepter les souffrances et les recevoir comme
un don de Vous : que Votre Règne arrive!

O Fils, qui êtes Dieu, voici que je lève mes mains
pr. offrir mes souffrances comme un sacrifice par
Vous : que Votre Règne arrive!

O Esprit-Saint, qui êtes Dieu, voici que je lève
mes mains pr. offrir mes souffrances comme
un sacrifice par Vous : que Votre Règne arrive!

O Sainte Trinité, par Jésus, avec Jésus et en Jésus,
plaisent mes souffrances Vous rendre tout honneur et
gloire! Ainsi soit-il.

Accordez-moi, Seigneur, d'être pleinement de cette vocation
de la souffrance : rendez-moi digne de souffrir!
Vous m'avez donné un corps infirme et débile :
O Père, me voici pr. accomplir Votre Sainte

One of the numerous "pieces of paper" of the young Poor Clare:
An offering to the Holy Trinity.

The refectory of the monastery. Sister Mary
of the Trinity had her last assignment here,
being placed in charge of the refectory.

Jerusalem: the garden of the monastery.

Jerusalem: a corridor of the monastery.

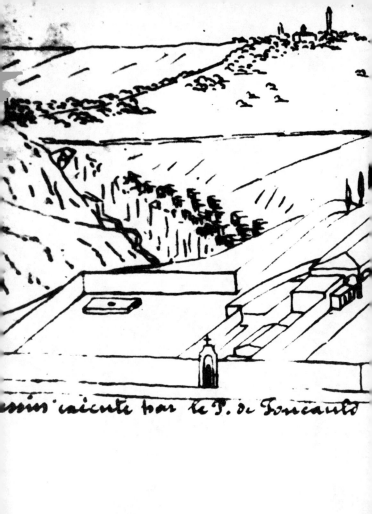

...ssin exécuté par le P. de Foucauld

The Monastery of the Poor Clares of Jerusalem. Sketch made by Father Charles de Foucauld (1858-1916); the Hermit of the Sahara spent several months in the service of the Sisters. It was in this retreat that, on the advice of Mother Elizabeth, Abbess of the Monastery, he decided to seek to enter the priesthood.

Above: The cemetery of the Poor Clares in Jerusalem where
Sister Mary of the Trinity was buried.
Below: The tomb of Sister Mary of the Trinity.

SR. MARIE DE
LA TRINITE
1901 - 1942

in My Eucharistic life, and I have made My manner of working imitable...To pray, to listen to Me, to bear all sufferings patiently, to keep silent so as to give place to charity...That is the Vow of Victim that I have asked of you." (Nos. 490, 519).

As with her life, so her death was, in a sense, Eucharistic. So gently, without anyone noticing it was this last coming of Jesus to Sister Mary of the Trinity. "Now, when receiving Me each morning in Holy Communion, it is you who absorb Me; at your death, it is I who will absorb you—to unite you to Myself." (No. 385).

After the death of Sister Mary of the Trinity, a spring breeze seemed to pass over the community. A renewal of fervor, an effort at cordiality and humility in fraternal life made peace and joy radiate on the faces, but especially in the depths of hearts.

Through the breath of the Holy Spirit, the message of Our Lord given through Sister Mary of the Trinity began to bear fruit there, then in other souls touched by her writings and whom her prayer would commend to the Lord Jesus.

— Part Two —

THE MESSAGE

INTRODUCTION

by Father Duboin

At the beginning of January, 1940, Sister Mary of the Trinity began to write down in a little notebook some interior words. Ever since the February night of 1926 [when she had seen the mysterious nun], which overturned her life, peace no longer consisted for her in remaining in her present situation, but rather in conforming to what the Lord now wanted of her. But how was she to know it? Without ceasing, she asked through prayer; she learned to be silent, to listen in order to perceive a response. God has a thousand ways of making Himself understood. Ever more attentive, Louisa discerned more clearly the interior call, punctuated sometimes with explicit words. Nevertheless, it was not at those important moments when she had to make a decision: she sensed herself then alone, free, and responsible for her choices. But before or after, this voice gave her courage and urged her—especially to go right up to the gift of herself in the cloistered life.

Attention to know the will of God is the fundamental attitude of the interior life. It is the teaching of the Bible, from the *"Schema Israel"* ("Hear, O Israel") of Deuteronomy and the calls of the prophets, right to the words of Jesus Himself, as reported by Saint John in the discourse after the Last Supper or in the Apocalypse: "If any man shall hear my voice, and open to me the door, I will come in to him, and will sup with him, and he with me." (*Apoc.* 3:20).

137

Sister Mary of the Trinity also found confirmation of her experience in reading the mystics. At the beginning of this same year, 1940, on the occasion of the week of prayer for Unity among Christians from the 18th to the 25th of January, she wrote to her friend Lydia von Auw, then pastor of a Protestant church in the canton of Vaud: "I think of you still more when we have Holy Hours of Adoration in front of the Blessed Sacrament. . . Before God everything is quiet, everything effaces itself, except what He Himself has engraved on our hearts, and then the words of the saints make themselves understood little by little by this poor sinner that I am. 'To know oneself, to know God!'

"You know the saying of Blessed Angela of Foligno [with regard to speaking about anything other than God]: 'How tiresome it is to speak in order to say something else! Silence, silence on everything which is not that. . .' And the words of the Lord to Saint Angela: 'If someone wanted to see Me, I would uncover My face with joy. If someone wanted to feel Me in his soul, I would not withdraw from him; if someone wanted to converse with Me, we would speak together familiarly with immense joy.' I am sending these words to you because I love them.

"Recently we read a very simple and beautiful book entitled *Un appel a l'amour* [*The Way of Divine Love*, TAN Books], the message of a little lay Sister Josefa Menendez, whom Our Lord asked to write what He communicated to her: the call of His love and of His mercy."

Did this reading incite the Sister to begin to note down also a heard message? Her intentions seem more modest; she wrote for herself, to hold her own during the arid days. (cf. No. 163). She was especially far from thinking that the hearing of interior words is something exceptional. A few weeks later, they were reading in the refectory the life of Sister Mary of the Divine Heart [Blessed Maria Droste zu Vischering], of the Good Shepherd nuns at Angers, where it was also a question of the interior voice of the Lord. On this subject, Sister Mary of the Trinity one day asked her Mother Mistress:

"And you, Mother Mistress, have you often heard the voice of the Lord?"

"No, at least, I don't know, I don't remember. And you, have you heard it?"

"Yes, sometimes."

She noticed that this response made an impression on the Mother Mistress, which rather surprised her. In fact, she was persuaded that the Lord talks to each soul as He talked to hers. Later, when the confessor who reported this dialogue,[1] Father van den Broek, tried to explain to her that the Lord can speak in different ways, and therefore if He speaks to each soul, He does not necessarily speak to each one in the same way, Sister Mary of the Trinity seemed not to understand. A little while later, she came back to the subject and declared to him: "Listen, Father, the Lord does not agree with you, He told me again, and He insisted that He speaks *to each soul.*"[2]

The confessor did not doubt her sincerity, but he feared illusion for her. It was then that he asked her to write down these words and to submit them to him regularly. As the witness in the best position to judge the common sense of the Sister, he was especially impressed by her fidelity in answering the least calls of grace. After the death of Sister Mary of the Trinity, he made it his duty to publish these Notebooks, which appeared to him to be a "message."

Certainly this type of communication should be received with prudence. Without contradicting this desire and the possibility of the interior dialogue, Saint John of the Cross shows how much discernment is important and delicate: "It is not rare to see scarcely recommendable people who, because they have heard interior words on the occasion of a meditation...baptize them right away as divine communications and, completely convinced, go about proclaiming: 'God told me this, God told me that.'"[3]

On this point, contrary to many warnings attributed to the Lord or to the Virgin Mary and spread about in these troubled times, the Notebooks of Sister Mary of the Trinity present themselves first of all as a demanding and very concrete directory of Christian life and of docility to the Church. They address themselves to the Sister herself and to souls who, whether in the cloister or in the world, are all called to follow the path of holiness. (cf. *Lumen Gentium*, chapter 5).

How did the Lord talk to His servant? Father van den Broek, her spiritual director and the first editor of her writings, gave this response: "As the *Imitation* says: without the sound of words."[4]

Sister Mary of the Trinity often asked herself about the nature of this interior voice. She answered her confessor's questions, as in this passage from a letter which should secure our attention: "...after that, He was quiet. But when He is quiet, it is as if He were still speaking. He makes you understand.

To try to say it in words is like a caricature."

The Notes, many of which are of high quality, disclose in their entirety a very profound faith. If one may come across some naive lines and a few awkward passages, one must understand that the mind of the Sister when applying the thought of faith to the concrete events of her life did not benefit from special assistance. Moreover, there is the work of writing it down, which is not infallible in the choice of words. That is why, in these Notebooks, the authority which one can attribute to the words of Jesus does not go beyond that of the contemplative religious who wrote them.

Yet if we keep in mind her message as a whole, we are impressed on seeing how much it was directed toward the future and with what vigor it always calls us to a personal and communal renewal.

May the reading of these lines bring forth in us the desire to know more about them, and especially to practice interior silence in order that we may listen for the Master.

NOTES

1. Rev. Silvère van den Broek, O.F.M.: *Soeur Marie de la Trinité*, second edition, Malines, 1947-1948, p. 15.
2. See Nos. 137 and 247 [and 33].
3. Saint John of the Cross: *The Ascent of Mount Carmel*, Book II, ch. XXVII.
4. *Imitation of Jesus Christ*, Book III, ch. 2.

— 1 —

THE MESSAGE AND THE MESSENGER

This chapter is the work of Father van den Broek, Father Duboin, and the Poor Clares of Rockford.

"JESUS—LISTEN TO HIM!" These words, spoken to Sister Mary of the Trinity during the retreat preceding her Vow of Victim, explain the existence of the Notebooks. "I speak to each soul. I attract all souls to Myself. I invite them...Many do not hear; many do not listen. I who never disappoint you am unceasingly disappointed...Give Me your blood—will you?—you who love Me, that I may trace in letters of fire these few words for which souls are waiting: 'Jesus—listen to Him!' " (No. 137). Sister Mary of the Trinity lived this listening to the Lord.

At the end of her first Notebook is a lengthy communication which she entitled "History." Although the opening lines have been referred to previously, it appears advisable to reproduce here in its entirety this unique document—the inner spiritual journey of a person as seen by God.

"You came to ask Me for help through My Sacraments. My grace resuscitated you.

"And immediately, one right after the other, I asked great sacrifices of you. Then you began to love Me. You loved Me ardently, wanting to give Me all

142

your strength, all your time, all the affection in your heart, every breath of your life. And you emptied yourself out, you emptied yourself out . . .

"But you were not satisfied, and your gifts did not make you rich. Then I asked you to follow My desires, to give in to them, to conform your life to them whatever the cost.

"And the trials and happiness came, because I was singing for joy in your docile soul. Now, you no longer leave Me and you listen to Me always. It is as if you gave Me great treasures, and I read in your heart this passionate desire to make all souls know that I am in them, so close, speaking to them. I, the friend, the consoler, the guide, the source, the God of their destiny . . . It is sufficient for them to be very silent to discover the voice of Jesus. Yes, I will send them this message, and I will write it with your blood."

At first Sister Mary of the Trinity only took down certain notes which she judged most useful to console and sustain herself in the days of trial which every soul must expect. Later her confessor told her to write down more and to submit to him what she had written. Jesus refers to these Notes and then requests: ". . . now write for Me what I tell you." (No. 163). This is the reason for the communications: "I do not speak to you in order to give you consolations, but in order that you may write what I tell you." (No. 192).

The first thing the Sister was to write was the story of her conversion and vocation. This was to be accomplished rapidly, leaving her free for the work Jesus desired of her, to write ". . . more important messages." (No. 510). Faithfulness to this request made demands on her and was to be the source of certain interior and exterior difficulties. These very problems would be occasions for the Master of the work to reveal Himself.

Within the exacting framework of the monastic schedule of alternating work and prayer with rare free moments available, where was she to find the time? That this was not always easy can be gathered from the appeal: "...do not let a single day pass by without having written at least one thing that I have told you; that is the alms you give Me, by believing My words." (No. 356).

Jesus took the matter in hand, first by counseling calmness. "You must do one thing at a time—you must write one thought at a time, one after another, as rapidly as your schedule permits, in an orderly way, as I present them to you at the time..." (No. 285). She is reminded that "Your first duty now is to hold yourself ready, and to listen to Me. I have placed you in circumstances that will allow you to listen to Me without in any way neglecting your work. Soon you will also have more opportunities to write what I tell you." This would be accomplished by a change of duties. "You have been given work that requires no personal initiative, no effort on your part, so that you can be entirely given up to what I say to you. I ask that of you now. The only thing that I ask of you now is to write what I say to you— would you refuse Me that?" (No. 344).

No, the Sister would not refuse, but she would become alarmed. One day the realization struck her that what she had been asked to write might come into the hands of others. This caused her much distress. Our Lord calmed her in His own way. "Yes, write what I tell you—write for souls; then trouble no more about what you have written. If it is good that others should read it, I will see to it. Write for souls and for Me." (No. 179). This same watchful care for the communications is revealed in two other notes. ". . .but My words will remain, those that I wish to remain—it is I who will see to it." (No. 543). Often interrupted in the midst of her writing by the bell summoning her to some community exercise, the Sister could not always complete the thoughts she had been transcribing. She was not to be concerned over this, but to write ". . .without worrying about those you only half remember. I will recall them to your mind if it is necessary." (No. 285).

Did Sister Mary of the Trinity herself have doubts concerning the reality of these interior communications? Yes, this was a struggle for her. Her confessor commented on it. The Notes themselves refer to it. "Yes, it is I who speak to you, even though you doubt it—I have already given you several proofs; I will give you more if you obey Me in all that I tell you—blindly. —With your Father's control, if necessary. You deprive yourself of graces when you do not listen to what I say to you. I have *My own* reasons which I do not always tell you." (No. 390). The confidence required of the Sister and its place in the communications is further revealed: ". . .So when you doubt, you think alone, your thought is no longer pervaded by Mine." (No. 252). The very simplicity of the interior words troubled the Sister: "You are still astonished that I only say ordinary, quite simple things to you, which everyone knows! I am more simple than you—yes, I the Eternal

Wisdom." (No. 271). "Because I say only simple things, and always concerning what is happening to you and what you see, you think it is yourself who suggest these thoughts." With a gentle touch of humor is added: "My little daughter, you would say more complicated things to yourself, as you used to do in your meditations." (No. 274).

It is instructive to comment on the words, ". . .with your Father's control. . ." quoted above. This is a prerequisite for the message. When the Sister is told that the interior Voice speaks to her in order that she may write, it is only, and very importantly, ". . . because your Father has accepted the charge of you; had he refused, I could not speak to you as I do—your imagination would be without control." (No. 192). The danger of being without control lies in the ruse of the devil: when he "cannot tempt you to do that which offends God, he strives by every means to diminish the good you could do, often to destroy it, by flattering you with illusions. Illusion is his chief means of spreading falsehood. To avoid those illusions, courage is needed—yes, courage. . .to receive the advice of those who direct you and to carry it out. That is why I wish you to submit what I say to your Father, even if it is disagreeable to you—I desire it." (No. 351). The use of the plural form of "you" indicates a warning meant for all.

What was it that the God who is Love so wished to communicate to souls? There is the call to the victimhood of "imitating My Eucharistic life." This aspect is explained in the following chapter, as well as in the Preface of *The Spiritual Legacy of Sister Mary of the Holy Trinity*. Here is offered another element, drawn from the Notes.

The Eucharist and the Redemption are intimately related, and each is intended for every single individual. The immense importance which the Lord attaches to *each* person and His plans for the happiness of each are touchingly revealed in many of the Notes. "God is more simple than you. It seems to you that I am always repeating the same thing: all religion and all your happiness consist in a few words of the Gospel which it is sufficient to understand and to practice. *'Seek first the Kingdom of God and His Justice; and the rest will be added unto you!'*" (No. 173).

"Ah, if you understood! How happy each soul could be in My intimacy!...I give Myself to all souls; but I have secrets to give each one that are for her alone, with her mission which is hers alone...The soul that understands this lives in complete contentment in doing My will and in receiving My Word with My confidence. Write that, perhaps one or other soul will read it and will understand it." (No. 169).

"I wish *each soul* to understand that she is dear to Me in a special way—that she has her own place in My Heart which no one else can replace. That she has her own mission which no one else can fulfill like herself. If she refuses, then that which only *herself* could have done, will not be done. Write that.

"I wish *each soul* to understand that My omnipotent Love transforms all that which you give Me, working wonders with it for Eternity. But if you do not give Me that which is left to your free generosity, I, who can create worlds, cannot do that which was entrusted to your initiative, if you refuse Me your human cooperation. Write that.

"I wish *each soul* to understand how great and unique is *her own* destiny. Write that.

"If each religious soul understood that My love *has need* of her, that I am waiting for her in the shadow and silence of her soul, to live a secret and wholly interior life with her, her happiness would be complete. Then there would no longer be any weariness, sadness, irritation, boring monotony, or routine in My service. I make Myself so small, I am so near you...but they do not want to believe that My Divinity hides Itself under the appearances which I have chosen...The soul that has found Me within her has all she desires and welcomes My Spirit; she listens to Me, she aims only at listening to Me, and accepting Me. Then everything becomes of use to her, and to be turned to account—everything becomes precious to her—everything becomes to her a gift of God and life. Ah, if every soul understood it! Write that." (No. 184).

Sister Mary of the Trinity had been told concerning the Message: "I will write it with your blood." "Give Me your heart—and your heart is your whole life." (No. 349). The words entrusted to her pen were first of all to be written by her life. "I wish each one of your days to be a picture of what I say to you. It is thus that I wish to speak through you." (No. 539). Her life was to give credibility and permanence to the Message. "Words have no efficacy in themselves, it is he who speaks them that gives them their sense and their power. If you live My words, they will be understood by other souls, they will not fall into oblivion. See, I confide them to you. Be faithful." (No. 199). The Sister understood, and accepted, her participation in the Divine plan:

"...I feel, I *know*, O my God, that You will bring to pass, beyond all that I can imagine, my immense desires for union among souls of good will for Your glory! I will intercede until the end of the world. It will be You who will work." (No. 541). "It is then that I shall begin to do good on earth, because it is *You* who will send me!" (No. 520).

"Let your light shine before men so that they may glorify your Father in Heaven" we are told in the Gospel. Brought "out of darkness into His marvelous light," Sister Mary of the Trinity, true daughter of Saint Clare—whose very name means light, the shining one—was destined to bear in her very person radiant testimony to the work of God.

"I do not speak like you, using phrases; I am Spirit and action; I speak in actions. Learn to read My thoughts, My desires, and to imitate My actions...

"Tell your love in actions; tell your vows in actions—unceasingly bearing witness to them in the little actions of each moment.

"Tell your hope and your joy in actions.

"Tell your faith in action.

"It is thus that the light that has been entrusted to you will shine before men." (No. 183).

If every soul would take these words to heart, each fulfilling her destined role, then the glory of God would be visible upon earth! "If each soul thus made that portion of the light which has been entrusted to her 'shine before men,' the House of Light, which is the Church, would become irresistibly resplendent..." (No. 183).

— 2 —

THE VOW OF VICTIM

This summary is taken from Father Duboin's Index in Qu'un meme amour nous rassemble.

This call to be "victim," the idea of making it the object of a vow and the insistence with which this step is requested of Sister Mary of the Trinity, occupies a very important place in the message. How shall we understand it?

A brief synthesis of the Notes shows that it involves offering oneself as a "voluntary victim" in order to participate with the Saviour in the work of expiation of sins: Nos. 21, 80, 86, 100-102, 110, 114, 131, 165, 330. Successive calls addressed to Sister Mary are given in Nos. 51, 61, 100-103, 105.

What is requested of generous souls is *silence,* listening rather than speaking—*a state of interior poverty,* before men as well as before God, without pretension, while interceding ceaselessly in order to obtain from God the triumph of Truth—*to overcome evil with good,* demanding nothing from others but supporting all the "stripping away" without defending oneself, offering at each chance an act opposed to the evil which one has seen: 363, 366, 418, 430, 457, 529, 634, 658, 661.

The model of this offering is *the Eucharistic life* of the Lord. Through this completely given presence, Jesus perpetuates among us His adoration and His intercession in silence, in His obedience and His dependence, to spread His Spirit and to hasten the coming of His reign.

This offering makes one enter into a life of intimate union with the Saviour: "It is the lambs who know Him and who hear His voice." See 61, 80, 86, 100, 165, 363.

Sister Mary of the Trinity is invited to pronounce this offering in the hands of Mary: 110, 363. As a "Vow of Victim," or under other formulations, this call to voluntary reparation for sin in union with the Saviour has always been heard in the Church. Besides, it has a biblical foundation, starting with the prophetic messages of Isaias and Jeremias (the Lamb, the Servant of God) right up to the invitations of the Epistles (for example, *Romans* 12:1). From the first martyrs to the mystics of our days, under the inspiration of grace, generous souls have followed the Lord right up to the greatest proof of love: "to lay down one's life for those that one loves." (*John* 15:13). Often this gift has found its model in the Eucharist: "I am the wheat of God and I am ground in the teeth of beasts to become the immaculate bread of Christ." (St. Ignatius of Antioch). St. Francis of Assisi, contemplating the Eucharist, wrote in his "Letter to the Entire Order"(29): "Therefore hold back nothing of yourselves so that He who gives all of Himself to you may receive all of you." The Notes of Sister Mary of the Trinity illustrate in a particular way this imitation of the Lord in His Eucharistic life.

TEXTS

(The following are the principal Notes referring to the Vow of Victim, with their numbers as in The Spiritual Legacy of Sister Mary of the Holy Trinity. *The Notes reproduced here are only those of broad, general import. Others related to the Vow of Victim in the spiritual life of the Sister can be found in that book: Notes 21, 80, 100, 101, 103, 110, 114, 131, 418, 634.)*

86. "Yes, there is a multitude of victims who save Love and Justice from destruction. Those who are passive victims glorify Me by their patience in bearing the consequences of sins which they have not committed—by their charity which makes reparation and pardons.

"But those who offer themselves voluntarily to make expiation, glorify Me more; they give Me the greatest proof of love. They are My sheep who know Me and who know My voice..."

102. "There must be victims who mingle their blood with that of Calvary—that is Justice, that is Order, that is Divine Wisdom, and the demands of Sanctity.

"There must be victims who bear witness to My Word, in order that it may be transmitted as a living thing and that it may be accurately perpetuated..."

165. "If there were more voluntary victims, there would be fewer involuntary victims who are obliged to submit to the terrible consequences of sins which they have not committed.

"I desire an army of victims who offer themselves

voluntarily to suffer the heavy chastisements that the world has brought upon itself by turning away from God.

"These victims know Me and unite themselves to Me by choosing Calvary in order to follow Me.

"But the chastisements that fall on the whole universe strike a multitude of souls who are not prepared to suffer injustice and who are in danger of losing their love and faith.

"I desire an army of voluntary victims who, in order to save souls, bring Me the help that the world refuses Me."

330. "I desire a great multitude of victim souls. But I do not confide the same mission to all of them. Nevertheless all must reproduce something of the life of the Man of Sorrows so that it may be kept alive and passed on among you."

363. "I desire an army of apostolic souls consecrated to Me by the vow of victim, not to expiate the sins of others by extraordinary trials; no, that is not My desire.

"I desire a great army of victim souls who will join Me in the Apostolate of My Eucharistic Life, who bind themselves by the Vow of Victim to choose the methods which I chose:

"silence—immolation—radiating the triumph of the life of the Spirit,

"so that My Spirit may spread and so that they may reveal something of My Kingdom, where every soul is called and awaited.

"I desire an army of victim souls who will confine their efforts to imitating My Apostolate:

"I am the Master: I have been the servant of all.

"The Vow of Victim will give them the strength of a greater fidelity to be the servants of all—so that My Spirit may spread and the world may believe My words.

"I desire these victims to be everywhere: in the world and in the cloisters; in every occupation, in every station of life, in the fields and in factories, in schools and in stores, in families and in convents, in business and in the arts, everywhere. . . so that their fidelity may bear witness to My words.

"Souls who offer themselves as victims are much more closely united to Me—the more I love a soul, the more I desire to associate her with My apostolate—look at My Saints and look at My Mother. . .

"Then I can ask of them—and I can give to them. . ."

366. "I ask four things of the souls who bind themselves more closely to Me by the Vow of Victim:

"1) to listen to Me more than to speak to Me;

"2) to strive to reproduce My actions—My way of acting rather than My words;

"3) to be before men as they are before God in a state of poverty that begs—not in a state of spiritual wealth that gives alms of its superfluity. . .

"Poor souls, without pretensions, are in the truth, and because they are *true,* they do not hurt their fellow creatures, and My grace can work with them.

"Victim souls will beg more than they will give;

"4) to confine their efforts to spreading My Spirit, My gentleness, and My kindness which does not dwell on evil, but overcomes evil by good.

"By being exacting with no one but themselves, they will help souls, by their silence and their respect, to receive the graces which their fidelity and their sacrifices will obtain from God."

430. "Listen to My silence: it is thus that one worthily adores God.

"Look well at the Host—how frail it is! So is My grace. I am living there, an invisible but real Presence. So does your soul live in your body.

"I live there in a state of obedience,

of patience,

of dependence,

so should all souls live who are vowed to religion, and all victim souls.

"Tirelessly day and night I intercede before the Father and I attract souls: so should you live in the tabernacle which is your convent."

457. "The state of victim is to bear without defending oneself, as I did in My Passion, insults, slander, mockery, brutality—to allow yourself to be stripped, yes, even to nakedness. You will never have all that; but accept the acts of self-stripping that solicit your generosity. . ."

458. ". . . Souls of goodwill are needed, and without great exterior show,

"souls entirely surrendered to the action of grace through the Sacraments,

"entirely surrendered to the redemptive action of the Cross,

"entirely surrendered to the invisible and powerful action of the Holy Spirit,

" 'victim' souls, united to the Victim of Calvary and of the Altar, not passively, but like Him, following Him...

"That is sufficient..."

529. "Yes, I ask for an army of Victims, scattered everywhere—for everywhere evil is mingled with good: in the organization of states as in that of communities, in families as in each soul.

"I ask that those who love Me should offer themselves as *victims* to make reparation by overcoming evil by good in the environment in which they find themselves.

"That they consecrate themselves to that reparation by imitating that which I pursue in My Eucharistic life:

"by silence;

"by offering Me on every occasion an act contrary to the evil they have seen;

"by exacting nothing from others, but from themselves;

"by obtaining from God the triumph of truth..."

658. "See, do I trouble Myself about the insults that are unceasingly heaped on Me? No, I make reparation—I wait for souls, I wait until they understand, until they repent, until they come to Me.

"A victim soul must conform herself to My Eucharistic Life..."

661. "What I ask of you, what I expect of you, is that you act not by becoming irritated or by speaking, but according to My way of acting, by imitating My Eucharistic Life.

"That is the Vow of Victim that I have asked of you.

"Take courage. I will so greatly bless your efforts that many souls after you will hasten the coming of My Kingdom by using the same means that I have indicated to you.

666. "You see, My little daughter, they wish to give themselves to Me, but they cannot join a religious order, so what is to be done?

"I want souls to know that by the Vow of Victim they enter into a life of union with Me.

"They must know that I ardently desire this Vow of Victim.

"It is thus that society will be reconstituted.

"They must know that the Vow of Victim means: *to imitate My Eucharistic life.*

"I desire that there be some of them everywhere, in every state of life.

"You will offer Me much—on account of your Vow of Victim, and by your Vow of Victim—in order that souls may understand its urgency.

"I greatly desire this Vow of Victim, wherever there are generous souls."

WORDS OF OUR LORD TO SISTER MARY OF THE HOLY TRINITY

These extracts from the Sister's "Notes," taken from The Spiritual Legacy of Sister Mary of the Holy Trinity, *were selected and arranged by Sister Mary Gabriel, P.C.C. (Colettine Poor Clare). They constitute a small sampling of Our Lord's words on various topics. As in the rest of this book, the words "you," "yours" and "your" are underlined when they are a translation of the French plural* vous. *Cf. p. 125.*

THE LOVE OF THE HOLY TRINITY FOR MEN

240. "...Ah, if you knew how the Holy Trinity watches over you! You are lost, carried in its solicitude as a child in the womb of its mother, and like that child you are unaware of your happiness. Open your understanding to the ceaseless messages which reveal it to you..."

611. "...My little daughter, you belong to the Holy Trinity.

"The Father created you to give you the Son, who redeemed you to give you to the Father, and to the Holy Spirit who transforms your soul.

"My little daughter, you participate in the life of the Holy Trinity by grace working in you, through

158

the Sacraments—and by your state of obedience depending on God. The Holy Trinity gives itself to its creatures, it deigns to give itself to you...but it is I who speak to you."

CHRIST'S LOVE FOR US

5. "You are Mine—you are altogether Mine... Do not go away. Stay with Me, *in* Me who never leave you. I have waited so long for you.

"This is the only reality: *I love you and I take care of you*. And that is for now and for eternity.

"Everything else must be borne with meekness and patience. They are only fleeting shadows which pass around you. But I remain. I love you and I take care of you."

168. "Yes, I attend to these details of your life—you are amazed at it! As a mother interests herself in all that concerns her newborn infant, I interest Myself in all that affects you. I do not lower Myself by doing so because I am not a degree of greatness, I am Love, and Love remains great when manifesting itself among little things as well as among great things."

169. "...I am as near you as your own breath, and you seek Me so far away in formulas and attitudes outside of you!

"Ah, if you understood! How happy each soul could be in My intimacy! The pettinesses that *blind* you would, of themselves, disappear in this ever growing quest for Love—and I am Love, I who answer as soon as I am called...I give Myself to all souls; but I have secrets to give each one that are for her alone, with her mission which is hers alone...

"The soul that understands this lives in complete contentment in doing My will, and in receiving My Word with My confidence. Love carries her: she lives. She experiences joy, and the gift of self. She lives in Me, and wants for nothing.

"Write that; perhaps one or other soul will read it and will understand it."

278. "My little daughter, I have loved you as no one else has done...I have wished not only that you should share My happiness in Heaven, but I have wished to give you My own life...Strive to live as I did. Love all. I loved even My executioners and I gave Myself up to their fury to obtain their pardon through My blood—the salvation of those souls created for Love and who did not know Love. Love all, all that is not adverse to My action—and in all that happens to you love My hidden will, which seeks to draw you nearer to Myself.

"With ruins, on ruins, I can build magnificently. It gives Me joy to use that which has humbled itself before Me, because My action is free.

"To submit to My action, to receive it without altering it, and to correspond with what it asks, is proof of true love.

"It is a still greater love to call forth My action by the intensity of your prayer.

"I always grant what you ask for the good of your soul: open your eyes—take it!"

491. "In God, you find no regret of the past; all is enveloped in the present—wherein His love consumes all bitterness and changes redemptive suffering into joy.

"Stay near your God—then you will know how to love your neighbor..."

513. "Do not think about the difficulties in the house. There is only one reality: I love you. You are Mine."

551. "Give Me your heart—the heart which creatures do not know and which they slight; it is more than a universe to Me, because I love you.

"It is all I ask of you.

"If you give it to Me, I will make it My Kingdom."

THE HOLY SPIRIT

301. "Truth makes no noise, but nothing will ever destroy it; that which *is*, lives on.

"It does not seek to crush its obstacles, to shine in a dazzling manner... It is often hidden by falsehood, but it lives on within, within circumstances and creatures, like inextinguishable embers, and in the end its light always breaks through obstacles—nothing can extinguish truth.

"My Spirit works in the same way within your souls, imperceptibly; He does not seek to triumph by blasting all that opposes Him, but like an interior light in the end He shines through all.

"He is as powerful as the most violent winds which He controls. He breathes where He will, and if you allowed Him to work, He would transform your world. But He has made Himself your Servant.

"Is it not He who inspires your desires? And He waits for you to pray before answering your requests. As soon as you invoke Him, He is there. Although you often grieve Him, He never takes revenge. But

He cannot prevent you from suffering from the consequences of your actions. He waits till you come back to Him: His patience is indefatigable.

"Yes, My Spirit has made Himself your Servant. . .so that you may learn of Me to submit yourselves entirely to God."

577. ". . .The good Spirit, the Holy Spirit is like a breath of joy that carries everything along on its way. He is contagious. By His very nature He diffuses His joy as a rose gives its perfume. Give way to Him!

"He is ingenious. He suggests ideas to you that are always new and fruitful so that you may win hesitating souls and draw them after you. Listen to Him!

"He is powerful; He strengthens those whom He animates. Thus those who are strong must support and carry in their arms more feeble souls."

604. "Live in My love—keep My Spirit.

"My Spirit is your strength, your joy, your light. It is your life. . .

"It is not difficult to keep it: be faithful to your duty, in *everything*. If you have done wrong, if you have had a blameworthy intention or thought, it is enough to acknowledge it and to ask for the pardon that makes reparation. Then you keep My Spirit and I live in you. . ."

608. "All souls could rapidly attain to the plenitude of their sanctity if they allowed Me to act, without resisting.

"Oh, the unacknowledged reserves of selfishness

which paralyze the omnipotence of the Holy Spirit within you!"

HOLY COMMUNION AND
THE INDWELLING OF CHRIST

18. "...I seek a heart whose love for Me is boundless,

"a will fused in My Will,

"a spirit so devoid of selfishness that My Spirit can take possession of it, and reign there as King...

"Will you be that heart, that will, that spirit?..."

29. "...I am your life. Do you understand that? I am as inseparable from you as your breathing, as the breath within your soul. I am so near to you.

"It is I who incline you to be patient, to be gentle, to accept things...Ask all of Me, ask every day, every morning what is necessary for the day, for yourself and for the human race..."

99. "Let Me act...

"and let yourself be fashioned...

"Oh, if you would leave Me to act; I would splendidly transform each one of your lives. But you oppose Me by your desires, your tastes, your resistance. My omnipotent Love is limited by the limit of your generosity."

116. "I continue to give My Body to the human race, to give it My Spirit, My Thoughts, ...the best of My Thoughts...

"Do you understand that? God's Thoughts are given to man!

"Not only do I give them to him, but I inspire

him so gently with them that they become his own, as part of his being; so that he may resemble Me and please God, I adorn him with one of the Splendors of Christ: His Thoughts! That is Love."

143. "I am living in the Blessed Sacrament, in the Real Presence...

"I, the Real Presence, am also living in each soul that is in a state of grace. Then why do you not, in spirit, adore My Presence in your neighbor?

"Your neighbor is always I, I who am asking of you or giving to you. The Holy Trinity is there in his soul. And if it has been driven out by sin, help your neighbor to receive it back by treating him as if I were already dwelling within him."

311. "See how My Presence is light, not encumbering, as delicate as it is faithful....

"I have reduced Myself to practically nothing so that I may live among you without being burdensome...Without the least trouble you can absorb Me, and I act within you, so utterly effaced that it appears as if it is you who act...That is true activity, that which lasts forever. Few understand it; they prefer visible action with its immediate results. Choose between them."

314. "To let Me live within you is to fill your heart with the utter surrender of little children—and to listen to Me. It is to apply all your intelligence to understanding My ways of working and to imitate them—it is to have the same feelings as I have and to share My wishes. It is to keep in the truth with all the strength of your will, cost what it may, at

every instant and on every occasion."

407. "Sanctity is to allow Me to live in you, and it is I who bring it to pass within you. It is to give Me your human nature so that I may live on among you.

"It is simple. Children understand it."

490. "Yes, I am infinitely happy.

"I love to give Myself in Holy Communion—to communicate My life to souls. I so ardently desire to communicate My life to you!

"You see, to be better able to work in you, I make Myself small, so small, insignificant...

"So as to be able to communicate My Spirit better to those around you, would you be willing to make yourself small, quite small in your outward life, a mere nothing of no consequence, just an insignificant nonentity?..."

493. "When I come down in Holy Communion, I bring with Me the gifts of the Holy Spirit, and His virtues, all the virtues.

"I bestow them. It rests with you to assimilate them, to blend them with the substance of your soul by putting them into practice.

"I begin by offering you My meekness—then, when I have given you all, to end up with, the last of My gifts is again My meekness."

502. "Yes, it is I who comforted you in Holy Communion.

"I speak to you without your seeing Me: nevertheless, it is I.

"I unceasingly shower you with favors that you scarcely perceive, but from which you benefit: those are My gifts.

"I give Myself to you through the Eucharist, I mingle Myself with your life so as to transform it—I blot out your sins and repair their damage—I change your weakness into strength, I communicate My life to you...You are not aware of it; nevertheless you enjoy its benefits...."

514. "How can you receive the benefits of My Communion, if during the day you have not communed with each other by bearing your defects, by fraternal charity?"

521. "If you knew how I need to find souls who love Me, who have used their day in preparing to receive Me! If you knew! You would prepare your soul better."

525. "The best gift that you can make Me is to receive Me."

MARY THE MOTHER OF GOD

55. "...Think of My Mother, whom I have given to you to be your Mother also. Who was charged with heavier responsibilities than she? Yet she was always calm and smiling because I filled her whole soul."

110. "...You will not understand till you get to Heaven what you owe to My Mother, and the gift that was made you when I gave her to you to be your Mother. How impenetrable is the love of God, who

created for <u>you</u> the Virgin Mary, Mediatrix of all graces!"

210. "Look at My Mother: silent, self-effacing.

"What did she say? Only a few words of hers are known. She spoke in actions.

"What did she do? Her ordinary daily duty, without noise.

"She gave very great glory to God because she *was*. She was content to be what God wished her to be, and in the way He wished it.

"It is sufficient to be.

"Beware of keeping up appearances—of seeking to explain yourself, of justifying yourself, of making yourself known, if there has been some mistake. It is sufficient to be. That alone stands before God and before Eternity."

224. "My Mother's arms were tender and enfolding, protecting and always calm, like an immovable refuge.

"I seek for rest in tender and protecting souls—who remain calm in the midst of all sufferings in order that My Love may express itself, and unfold its immense wings...

"You ask Me for love; accept suffering for Me and for souls: then you will love; love will possess you."

237. "Yes, I have made Myself so truly <u>your</u> Brother that I have willed that <u>you</u> should have the same Father as I, and that My Mother should become <u>your</u> Mother.

"Love does not keep for itself those whom it loves, it gives them away...

"One must love, to be able to give—so that the Holy Spirit may triumph and spread...."

259. "It is when a soul forgives and is silent that she most resembles My Mother."

341. My Heavenly Mother said to me:

"My life was a succession of trials more incomprehensible than yours. Nevertheless, I always loved. Love never left my heart. I knew that the salvation of souls is bought by the Blood of my Son and by our tears—yes, the tears of the heart..." [This is the first and only communication of the Holy Mother of God to Sister Mary of the Trinity.]

402. "You understand a little better that My Mother and I were very different beings from you—in quality—because we were without sin.

"Nevertheless we lived among you like everyone else.

"We did the Father's Will, all His Will, and bore suffering without rebellion and without bitterness. Love never left our souls.

"Is it so difficult to do as we did? In whatever situation you may find yourselves?

"I ask nothing else of you, because I wish you to share My happiness."

LOVE FOR GOD

44. "I ask only for love. Ah, what are you doing about it...?"

68. "I passed through the world doing good—I brought peace, order, kindness, an easy kindness.

"I healed the sick; I forgave sins; I gave joy, true joy, tranquil joy.

"I brought the Beatitudes.

"I revealed God.

"It is because men do not know Him that they do not love God.

"You must reveal God. That is charity.

"You must not furiously wrestle with evil; you must overcome evil by good.

"Good always triumphs in its time."

69. "...I can do everything in a heart that loves Me; but if I am not loved, I am powerless. Those who do not love Me—it is because they do not know Me. Work to make Me loved...."

95. "Those who love Me a little, have a little confidence in Me.

"Those who love Me much, have great confidence in Me.

"Those who place no limit on their love have a confidence in Me without bounds or limit. I cannot disappoint them.

"You honor Me more by the confidence you show Me than by all that you could give Me.

"And notice, I respond at once by putting joy into the heart that honors Me with confidence."

191. "Yes, there are many souls who serve Me without receiving any consolation from Me—their fidelity in that state shows a very great love."

213. "As a rule, to do a little more than is required is to offer Me the perfume with the flower.

This little extra effort, being voluntary, can only be an expression of love: it is more precious than all the rest; and usually it is neither seen nor known by anyone; it is for Me alone that it is done; it is the perfume of the flower..."

257. "Time filled with love is time well filled. Love multiplies time. He who loves finds means of doing many things from the outpouring of his heart...."

270. "I wish every soul to understand that I am awaiting her. That beyond this life a boundless love awaits her, and that she must hasten...must purify herself to meet love, and let that be her one object. You must carry your light on high so that others may see it and follow it. Then it will light up your own path too."

435. "Yes, I the Almighty chose all that through love: the Passion, the carrying of the Cross, the Crucifixion, death, the Eucharist...

"In the face of that, what could you also do to humble yourself through love! You find nothing!

"If it happens that you are thought useless, that you are little liked, that you are not wanted, that your intentions are misunderstood, welcome with joy these opportunities of following Me on the path of silence and love.

"Happiness is yours; you can find Me with you at every moment, in every occupation that comes to you —and when you accomplish your duty fully, perfectly, you will find Me still more.

"Why do you seek Me elsewhere?..."

545. "It is not when everything is going well that you love Me. It is when everything is going wrong, and in spite of it your soul remains united to Me, peaceful, occupied only in diffusing a good spirit."

REVEALING GOD

408. "The value of your life lies in that God Himself has been confided to you so that you may hand down the knowledge of Him to the generation who will follow you—the true knowledge of Him, of which the Church is the depository.

"That is your responsibility."

"I work in the world, but I allow you to work. You can second My action, and you can thwart it.

"That is your responsibility."

409. "You must make religion loved, at all costs. Souls must attach themselves spontaneously to My Church through love—otherwise their practice of religion will be in vain.

"It is only that which souls experience and live through love that procures God's glory and their own salvation.

"My disciples must at all costs make themselves all things to all men, in order to win souls over to listen to them, and eventually to listen to Me."

THE CHURCH

63. "All disorder arises from not listening to the Church. People wish to live outside My Church, although I am there, I who am source and strength....

"And those who are in the Church forget to listen to Me.

"They look on Me as a master, I who am always,

unwearyingly at your service, answering your prayers, waiting, hoping that you will ask of Me the better gifts.

"When I incline towards you, My justice and My Holiness hide themselves; there is only My boundless love calling for yours, giving you confidence, hoping for your generosity...."

288. "The great evil of Protestantism is that it deprives so many souls of good will of an immense share of graces obtained through My Passion and which are conveyed to you through the Sacraments.

"Ah, how it limits My action in souls who do not seek Me further and do not 'follow' Me further because they believe that they have responded definitively to My call once and for all....

"The great evil of Protestantism is that error wears the mask of truth.

"Much courage and deep personal labor are needed to discover the mask, to reject it, then to come humbly to the Source of Truth, to ask for His light and His strength.

"*Let your light shine before men,*' in order that they may understand that your Church is Christ, is the Truth."

601. "Prayer will not do everything in bringing heretics back to the Church; it will be of no use if it does not help each of you to remedy in yourselves that with which heretics can rightfully reproach My Church....

"The Truth, all revealed Truth, is in the Church—does your life, in your actions and in your words, always conform to the truth? Ah, it is not by strangers that I am betrayed, it is by the members of My own family!

"When all the members of the Church live what they profess, those heretics who are souls of good-will will understand, will come to us!"

641. "The Truth is in the Church. To fail in truth is to fail the Church. The Church is I.

"When you conform to what the Church says, you live My life, you defend My cause.

"When you do not conform to what the Church says, you live your life, according to your interests.

"Who will take My cause in hand?"

LOVE OF OUR NEIGHBOR

77. "Often remind yourself that you are all beings in evolution, depending on My grace and depending also on one another. You are interdependent, responsible for each other; responsible for what you become.

"You are all composed of many elements. Not one is altogether good or altogether bad...The tares must be allowed to grow with the good grain."

78. "One must encourage the good grain by stimulating it, cultivating it, by neglecting to see that which is not good in it.

"When that is understood, antipathies disappear....

"In each one there is the presence of the Holy Trinity: and in each a distinct character which is 'she,' which God has given to her in creating her soul; each soul has her own beauty—and glorifies Him in her own individual way.

"When that is understood, jealousies disappear.

"Each soul has her own mission—special to herself; she must be helped to fulfill it, and to use the unknown reserves of love and generosity that God hides in each soul.

"If you understood that, there would indeed be a great stream of cooperation to hasten the coming of My Kingdom...."

128. "These are two very different things: when you are kind to a soul whom, at the bottom of your heart, you do not esteem; or when you use your kindness to seek and find the beauty hidden in a soul that you are not inclined to esteem."

175. "The great omissions against charity are to forget to love your neighbor and to forget Me. Ah, yes, to forget Me, Me!

"To love is not merely to perform material actions; they flow from love: but their source is in the heart.

"To love is to have feelings only of goodwill which do not stop at the creature—but which ascend to the Creator.

"To love is to have the spirit of Faith."

221. "As physical life needs order, peace, and a minimum of well-being—so the spiritual life *needs* to meet with goodwill and kindness—with disinterested human love to reveal Divine Love to it. That is the normal way, established by God. I have made you dependent on one another."

414. "Remember that, like yourself, your Sisters need to feel themselves loved; it is a necessity, because you are creatures in a state of evolution, and

you *need* the love of others in order to develop.

"I am not a being in evolution, I have no need of your love like a creature—but I have need of your love for one another so that I may live among you and communicate My life to you; yes, 'I am the Vine and you are the branches'. . ."

439. "It is up to you to contribute, to a great extent, in the souls of your brothers, to their refusal or acceptance of My call.

"Ah, how responsible you are for one another!

"If you have not the strength to strive for your own sake, strive through pity for the souls of others. . . ."

449. "You hinder the flowering of My life in your Sisters' souls when you cause them some displeasure or vexation: yes, it is I who suffer through it. In order that I may grow in souls, I need them to be at ease, without bitterness, in kind dispositions— and how can one make others good. . .except by lavishing kindness on them. . .?

"Do it for Me. I want your presence or help to bring them nothing but joy. . . ."

573. "Love clothes those whom it loves with a beauty that it actually communicates to them. It sees the defects but it does not stop there; it overcomes evil by good—it corrects the defects by a spontaneous generosity of the will seeking what is good.

"Love does not love on the grounds of perfection—it radiates and triumphs over selfishness without any other reason than My Presence within you. . . ."

614. "You must have compassion for souls who are

nearing their eternity. They must be helped not to
have a single bitter feeling, no suspicion of rancor, so
that the love of creatures, human love, may open their
heart to divine love and to its demands for sincerity."

627. "My little daughter, it is a small matter to
be kind to those who are kind to you—but to be
kind, very kind—for love of Me, to those who make
you suffer, is really to belong to My family."

81. "...However poor and useless your life may
be, you are responsible for the souls you know, whose
difficulties you know—and their lack of faith—and
their ignorance of your Jesus. You are responsible
in the measure in which you understand.

"All do not see the moral misery, the powerless-
ness of souls who are the captives of sin. But it is
the duty of those who see to come to their aid, cost
what it may.

"Do not doubt; with Me you can do all."

PRAYER

75. "*Thy Kingdom come!* When will you understand that it requires much greater sacrifices than
material sacrifices, more heartfelt prayers than those
recited by the lips?"

130. "To speak or to listen to Me are two differ-
ent kinds of prayer."
"My Lord Jesus, which do You prefer?"
"That which listens to Me."

137. "I speak to each soul—I attract all souls to
Myself. I invite them...Many do not hear; many

do not listen. I who never disappoint <u>you</u> am unceasingly disappointed...."

140. "Yes, those who seek, find, and I give to those who ask of Me. But I have the joy of satisfying beyond all her expectations the soul who does not express any desire and who awaits Me...

"When you ask graces of Me for yourself or for others, your capacity for receiving is limited to your requests—When you await Me, asking for nothing but Myself, there is no limit in your heart. As soon as a soul awaits Me, I come to her. I have innumerable ways of approaching and speaking to her...It is love that will make her discover My language."

232. "Each time that by kindness in word or deed, you encourage good understanding between <u>you</u>—mutual support and help—you contribute to the *unity* of My Church: 'That they all may be one.'

"Pray thus in acts."

WORK

71. "Listen, you must not attach great importance to natural activity. *'Without Me you can do nothing.'*

"It is the spirit of the world that desires natures who are 'organizers,' 'efficient,' as they say when praising them.

"It is easy to make a stir, to work in a visible, outward manner; it is very difficult to renounce oneself and to let Me work. And yet that is the only fruitful activity, which lasts throughout eternity.

"Rest in Me. Depend on Me..."

231. "...Act quickly, with precision. Let all your

material work be regulated by order, method, and promptitude, so that you may be free to give yourself more to the life of the Spirit.

"I await you in material work in which I have such need to be served with perfection...."

380. "...I have sufficient talents at My disposal; what I desire is the *soul* to make it My place of rest and of work, to live anew in it in humanity.

"Yes, My place of work, because a soul that would give herself to Me without reserve, how I would use her for the glory of God and of the Church, for the salvation of other souls, to a degree that you cannot imagine!

"My little daughter, give Me your whole soul!"

522. "Your works please Me in the measure in which they express your love.

"If you do them for the pleasure of using your talents, of turning out something good, for your own satisfaction, it is not wrong, but what do they give to your God?

"Your works please Me in the measure in which they teach you to know yourself and to conquer yourself..."

577. "It is in your heart that you must overcome evil by good.

"That is the first work I ask of you. It is difficult and great; but it is that which honors Me— which procures the Father's glory. 'God is a Spirit, and must be worshipped in spirit.'

"The second work that I ask of you is to help your neighbor in this interior work...By silence, the effacement of nature—example—radiating joy. . . ."

SUFFERING

64. "Happy are the families and convents that have sick members! Because by being visited, the sick safeguard the practice of gentleness and patience; they expiate; they bear My likeness, the image of Christ suffering in His Church. To comfort them in the spirit of faith is to perform a work of reparation in the Church—the reparation I expect from those who love Me.

"A house where there are no sick runs the risk of living more for itself than for Me."

105. "Love and suffering are inseparable. It is those whom I love most that I honor with trials—believe Me.

"If you do not love or if you no longer love, it is because you have not yet suffered for the person toward whom you feel indifferent. The more one has suffered for a soul, the more one loves it."

235. "A little effort and pain, then such a great reward—and already here below the reward of seeing love, generosity, and the Faith spread irresistibly, like a spot of oil. . .

"And when you are in pain, do you not feel that I am there, that it is I who sustain, who carry you? . . ."

504. "You have no great sufferings to offer Me; but little daily pains, if you gather them all together, are the streams that make a great river. I know them all; not a single offering is lost. . ."

DEATH

145. "Do you think that I will abandon you at the moment of death, you who are so miserable that you cannot live without Me...? As a mother embraces her newborn child, so will I enfold you in My love; because you are My tiny child, and I know that you cannot do without Me..."

174. "It is at the hour of death that you will understand how much I have loved you."

281. "...At death, before God, and for eternity, this alone will remain in your being: your love.

"And in the Hands of God, wherewith to weave your crown, there will be found nothing but what you have given Him."

385. "I have wasted all my time, I have squandered my life; so far I have done no good!"

"If you obey My voice, that is a great good; I will do the rest. Is it not I who have done everything in your life? I will continue to work in you in death and after your death.

"Now, when receiving Me each morning in Holy Communion, it is you who absorb Me—at your death, it is I who will absorb you—to unite you to Myself. What do you fear?..."

THE VIRTUES

523. "Humility is not words, attitudes, or actions. It is the courage to look your most hidden intentions in the face, it is the courage to acknowledge it if they are selfish, and to ask Me to purify you."

650. "There are several forms of humility: that which admits your nothingness, your unworthiness, speaks according to wisdom and truth. But it is also a form of humility not to speak of oneself, because one does not think of oneself; one thinks only of Me. I love that silence concerning oneself..."

325. "Little children do not have great temptations—their self-abandonment preserves them from great evils, and yet they grow as if molded with love.

"Oh, if you knew how to live like little children, holding My hand—acting without arguing, without talking, and without thinking about yourselves, oh, how you would discover Me at every step!"

312. "Gentleness, patience, joy;

"Gentleness, patience, joy;

"Gentleness, patience, joy...give Me these three things, in your external life—in your judgments—your thoughts—in your feelings.

"Gentleness is the fruit of Love.

"Patience is the fruit of Faith.

"Joy is the fruit of Hope.

"When these alone fill your heart, I will reign in it as King."

125. "It is not sufficient to say: 'My God, I have confidence in You!' You must make the interior act of freeing yourself from all anxiety, and rest on My Heart like the Apostle St. John at the Last Supper—yes, like St. John, the Beloved Apostle. I await this confidence from every soul..."

THE PURPOSE OF LIFE

223. "An act of pure love is a very great thing.

"Oh, if you understood that, you would not wish to learn anything else!

"A soul that has done nothing beautiful, but who has loved God and her neighbors much, who, abiding in love, has welcomed all that I have sent her, that soul has greatly honored Me. Her life will be of value for all Eternity; she has contributed to the advancement of My Kingdom."

— 4 —

LIVING THE LIFE OF THE GOSPEL: MORE WORDS OF OUR LORD

This chapter of additional excerpts from the Notes was compiled by the Poor Clares of Rockford.

Throughout the communications of Our Lord to Sister Mary of the Trinity it is apparent that His words to her reiterate and explain His teachings in the Gospels. Note 352 illustrates this:

352. "My little daughter, I live in souls as I lived on earth. If you wish to know what fosters My life in you, see how I lived, as shown in the Gospel narratives.

"Silence and simplicity. Penitential poverty and detachment.

"Union with God; Joy; complete fulfillment.

"I move in souls always doing good; I use the same means, the same manner of acting, and I have never contradicted Myself:

" 'Let the cockle grow with the good grain'. . .

" 'Overcome evil by good'. . .

" 'Love your enemies and those who wish you ill'. . .

" 'Do not quench the smoking flax'. . .

" 'Let your light shine before men'. . .

"And My Beatitudes as I lived them, so do I live them anew in every soul—

"likewise My commandment. . .

"I spoke in parables and I prayed to My Father.
"I still speak in souls"—

The following selections demonstrate the fact that
the Notes of Sister Mary of the Trinity echo the
Gospels. These particular Notes are divided into five
sections: explicit commentaries on Gospel texts; ex-
pansions on the Gospel theme of "great joy"; insights
into the roles of several persons mentioned in the
Gospels; "Little Parables" which Our Lord used to
instruct Sister Mary of the Trinity, in much the same
way as He instructed His hearers in Biblical times;
and messages of Jesus regarding His Sacred Heart
and love for us—certainly an echo of the central message of the Gospels.

COMMENTARIES ON GOSPEL TEXTS

52. "Ask Me for two graces for the common life:
to be indulgent with others, 'letting the tares grow
with the good grain,' the strength silently on every
occasion, without relaxing, to overcome evil by good."

77. "Often remind yourself that you are all beings
in evolution, depending on My grace and depending
also on one another. You are interdependent, responsible for each other; responsible for what you become.
"You are all composed of many elements. Not one
is altogether good or altogether bad...the tares
must be allowed to grow with the good grain."

71. "Listen, you must not attach great importance
to natural activity. 'Without Me you can do nothing.'
"It is the spirit of the world that desires natures
who are 'organizers,' 'efficient,' as they say when

praising them.

"It is easy to make a stir, to work in a visible, outward manner; it is very difficult to renounce oneself and to let Me work. And yet that is the only fruitful activity, which lasts throughout eternity..."

157. "...For terrible is the condition of an impenitent heart, I cannot penetrate it. It is not I who condemn it, it is he who willfully repels Me. Pray for the wicked, suffer and expiate for them. Ah, yes, make smooth the ways of the Lord!"

348. "...Silence; respect for all creatures, for the sake of Him who created them.

"Stripping oneself in the joy of giving.

"Patience.

"Love which obeys the Voice of God not in appearance, but from the depths of one's being, in complete adhesion to the divine will;

"love which is generous, which is humble enough to ask, and which gives what it receives;

"I need all that in order to live in a soul, to grow there, and to reign there.

"Then the grace flowing from My Sacraments works visibly, increases and radiates...

"It is for you to prepare the ways of the Lord."

398. "...You must be firmly united to Me, and to the will of God alone, and detached from all else—capable of adapting yourselves to all circumstances, all situations, all the demands of life, in order to help Me to penetrate everywhere: you must make yourselves all things to all men—'make plain the ways of the Lord'..."

296. "Yes, I wished to draw you to Myself. You are on the right path. Continue on it. Do not waste your time in bothering about what others are doing. *'Follow thou Me.'*"

361. "...I am always with you, in you and around you, and you do not see Me.

"The obedient soul, the soul that is in the state of obedience, has her eyes open to My Presence; without leaving it, she finds signs of it everywhere and My messages also, because she yields immediately to what I say to her....

"The soul that resists, suffers and exhausts herself by resisting, and because she is not rooted in Me, her suffering is not the kind which expiates and produces an increase of love.

"So much suffering is misdirected and lost! It remains shut up in your human limitations.

" 'I am the Vine and you are the branches'; bring everything back to Me; with that which you give Me, I will work miracles for eternal life!"

376. "I said I would draw all men to Me when I was lifted up from the earth. My little daughter, remember that and understand it. It was not in My hidden life or during My ministry that I drew all men to Me; it was after I had been lifted onto the Cross. It was a supreme and apparent destruction—yet a triumph of Love, of the Spirit of God.

"Do not be surprised if I invite those who are Mine to let themselves be destroyed by love."

391. "Remember what I said of the pearls that must not be thrown to swine. I do not waste My

gifts; when a soul receives My smallest gifts with gratitude and respect, then I can confer more on her.

"Gratitude is a special mark of those who are Mine."

342. "Because My demands are more spiritual—known only to God!—than visible, and My rewards are more spiritual than visible, hidden from the eyes of men, immediate satisfactions, visible joys are preferred to Me...

"I am banished from nations, banished everywhere.

"Nevertheless 'My words will never pass away' and My work also triumphs everywhere: a little leaven is sufficient to make the whole dough rise!

"Does My work triumph over everything in your heart?..."

429. "Your mind must open to My light.—

Your heart must open to My love.—

"See, My little daughter, I really have to send trials to those whom I love in order to wrench them out of the network of habits or of errors wherein you run the risk of burying yourself.

" 'The disciples are not above the Master': it is by the Cross that I saved the world."

433. "...The religious life is a serious undertaking—you must not give yourself to it by halves; it would be better to renounce it altogether than to give yourself to Me by halves.

"My words are true: 'He who puts his hand to the plough and looks back, is not worthy of Me...' 'If thine eye is to thee an occasion of falling, pluck it out.' "

571. "It is here in these places [The Mount of Olives and Mount Sion can be seen from the convent garden at Jerusalem] that I suffered and consummated My Passion.

"Here that I was laughed at by all, mocked, scoffed, betrayed—covered with insults and invectives—here that I gave all My Blood...*I*, your God, the Son of God.

"Do you understand what you have to do if you love Me?

"Do you understand what this means: 'to follow Me'...?"

578. "There are so many misconceptions and misunderstandings between souls of goodwill because you create for yourselves a too limited, a too narrow idea of God. The perfections of God do not exclude one another.

"Why do you wish to imprison God and what He asks in your own ideal, which varies according to place and time? What the Church tells you about God is sufficient to disperse all misunderstandings. Why are you not content with what the Church says? 'He who is not against Me is with Me.'

"God is life. And wherever life circulates, He shows something of His power, of His goodness, of His magnificence.

" 'In My Father's House there are many mansions.' "

219. "When I see those who love Me obey with difficulty, it humiliates Me; when prayer, when virtue costs them something, it humiliates Me; I who have said that My yoke is easy and My burden light!

"Serve Me with a heart that sings!..."

THE CALL TO JOY

"Follow Me..." and "Serve Me with a heart that sings!" This call to Joy resounds throughout the Notes, reflecting the Gospel as 'Good News of great joy." It is possible to trace the intimate links of Joy with hope, with love, with fidelity, with the Cross, and thus discover that Joy is an indispensable element of the way to God.

72. "You are nothing, but this *nothing* will be eternally happy because I shall keep you always near Me.

"Just as We are happy and *one* in the Most Holy Trinity, so do I ardently desire that all, all My creatures may be united in Our immense joy—all, all My creatures..."

622. "Some call the way that leads to My Heart 'Love,' others call it 'suffering.'

"Love without suffering does not lead to My Heart.

"Love and suffering are inseparable—inseparable in their growth, inseparable in their demands—indissolubly united; but there is a fruit which they infallibly produce, and which men often forget to name when they speak of the way that leads to Me. I will tell it to you, My little daughter, it is *Joy*. Keep in your heart this three-fold name of the way that leads to My Heart:

"Love—Suffering—Joy!"

312. "Gentleness, patience, joy;

"Gentleness, patience, joy;

"Gentleness, patience, joy... give Me these three things, in your external life—in your judgments—

your thoughts—in your feelings.

"Gentleness is the fruit of Love.

"Patience is the fruit of Faith.

"Joy is the fruit of Hope.

"When these alone fill your heart, then I will reign in it as King."

634. "...I desire your soul to be immolated, in imitation of My Eucharistic Life, in silence, in neglect, in the gift of yourself in Me—by ceaseless intercession, by welcoming every occasion for expiation, in joy.

"Joy is not inscribed on the Holy Eucharist: it bears the image of the Crucifix. But do you not feel My joy when you receive Me? I communicate it to you; I give it to you. I am the true Victim. Follow Me to Calvary and even to the Eucharist."

COOPERATION IN JOY

"Make smooth the way of the Lord. . ." The Lord is always ready to fill souls with His Joy, but they must be prepared to recognize this gift and be open to receive it.

268. "You feel great joy when someone brings you a considerable alms, and you do well: you must show your gratitude in giving them pleasure.

"But I come to you with My offering of poverty, with My Beatitudes; why are you not thrilled with joy in recognizing that I have come to you?"

193. "When a soul finds joy in that which I give, I increase that joy; she examines My gift, and marveling, discovers that I have given her more than was apparent.

"But when a soul does not know how to be content with the little I give her, it is in vain that she seeks Me elsewhere. This is one of the secrets of interior consolation: 'He that hath, to him shall be given'; do you understand that now?"

195. "It is I who give interior joy, but never without your cooperation. It begins in a very small way, like a senna seed; if you nourish it by accepting every occasion of joy that I send you, I make it fruitful; it may flourish exceedingly.

"There would be less dryness in souls if they gave more consideration to My gifts to them and to others—if they were content with the little that is given them, because a little is sufficient to reveal My immense love."

222. "In order to hear My voice, you must silence all other voices in your soul.

"Contrary to human powers which thrust themselves on others, I never intrude Myself on anyone; it is with gentleness that I offer My Spirit. If I am welcomed, I impart Myself more freely. I do not enter into conflict, into rivalry with the sources of human joy that attract you; I simply offer you the choice: Myself or the others...."

624. "If you linger here and there to glean natural joys, you no longer need supernatural joys—it is you who are the cause of their rarity.

"You must choose."

517. "...Create silence around you and within you. Surrender your desires. Adopt My desires and

My feelings—then My joy will visit you, even in the
darkest gloom. Then you will see the Kingdom of
God established in you and around you—and all the
rest will be 'added unto you'. . ."

593. ". . . Do not let pass a single opportunity to
give joy to your Sisters, to give them pleasure, without disregard to your Holy Rule, and My joy will
remain in you."

JOY IN DAILY LIFE

*"He who puts his hand to the plough and looks back
is not worthy of Me. . ." Living each moment for God,
giving whatever it is possible to give, is to go forward
without looking back, and to go forward in Joy!*

46. "It is such a great thing to belong to Me! What
does anything else matter to you? Be full of joy at
belonging to Me. I want you to be altogether Mine!"

112. "Let go of the joys of earth, do not think of
them; let them be indifferent to you—and I will make
you know other, better joys. . . ."

208. "Time that is filled with joy, with joy directed
toward God, is not lost time."

220. "I would rather see a soul give Me little but
with great joy, than see her give Me much, see her
consecrate to Me all that a human life can consecrate, but with sadness; sadness is like a regret."

304. ". . . My little daughter, you give Me more joy
through the quality of your offerings than through

the quantity—it is the quality which honors Me."

386. "To bear monotony, the tediousness of the same work coming round regularly, the absence of novelty, while keeping a joyful heart, is to honor Me—that is to conform oneself to My hidden life.

"To be joyous simply because I am with you, when you have no other reason for being so, that is to prove to Me that you love Me. . ."

THE JOYS OF GOD

"Without Me, you can do nothing. . ." In a touching manner the Notes reveal the sources of that which can be described as the Joys of God.

1. "Forget yourself! Do not occupy yourself with your spiritual or material needs. When you have all that is necessary, you deprive Me of the joy of taking care of you."

11. ". . .Thoughts, memories, plans, desires, anxieties—whatever they may be. Confide *all* to Me. It is My joy to respond as God to humble confidence."

29. ". . .Ask all of Me; ask every day, every morning what is necessary for the day, for yourself and for the human race. Ask ceaselessly, without wearying.

"It is My joy to answer! I always answer; but My answer is varied. You would understand it better if you knew how to live by faith."

126. ". . . Your joy is to strip yourselves and to be dependent on Me alone.

"My joy is to be able to prove to <u>you</u> the prodigality of My love."

140. "Yes, those who seek, find, and I give to those who ask of Me. But I have the joy of satisfying beyond all her expectations the soul who does not express any desire and who awaits Me..."

169. "It is I who inspire <u>your</u> desires and encourage <u>your</u> generosity so that it may increase them, in order that I may have the joy of fulfilling them...."

173. "...Listen, and receive My grace.

"When a soul receives it with great joy, I give it to her in abundance. It is My joy to give! And <u>you</u> will never exhaust My riches. My gifts are inexhaustible and always new....

"I am not exacting. Oh, My yoke is so easy and My burden so light! I ask for a sincere heart that acknowledges its faults and the source of its faults down to the most hidden movements of the heart— and that brings Me its needs, asking Me for help.

"It is My joy to help <u>you</u>! I can do great things for Eternity with a soul who unreservedly gives herself to Me, letting Me work in her; and each soul, each one, is called to that."

190. "As parents are happy in showing their love to their children, so it is My joy to make My love felt, to reveal it; I do it in a reserved manner, perceptible to those who are attentive to My Presence and who seek it..."

274. "...Souls brilliant with natural talents have disappointed Me more often than little people. Do you believe it? It is My joy to make Myself little with the little ones."

278. "...With ruins, on ruins, I can build magnificently. It gives Me joy to use that which has humbled itself before Me, because My action is free...."

284. "Formerly I spoke in parables. In the secret intimacy of the soul, I speak softly, for it is necessary that a soul should come to Me *of herself.*

"The more a soul is Mine, the more I can speak to her without restraint—that is My joy!..."

364. "Why do you fear death? Do you doubt Me?

"For your sins: see, here is My mercy.

"For your cares, your anxieties, your desires: here is My Providence.

"For your weakness: here is My Omnipotence.

"It is My joy to give you hour by hour sufficient strength, to have you entirely dependent on My love."

417. "That which gives Me joy is to see you applying yourselves to the perfection of the duty of your state without wishing for anything more.

"Then the happiness of the Blessed is already yours in part, because you find Me at once there, in the perfection of the duty of your state...."

426. "It is My joy to pardon.

"If pride prevents you from being sorry for your sins for your own sake, be sorry for them out of love for Me, so that I may have the joy of forgiving..."

436. ". . .When you are united among yourselves, you can obtain everything from God, because you have obtained from yourselves the most difficult thing. And I have the joy of giving rewards. . ."

508. "My beloved, you will also be persecuted and criticized. My love will cover you as an impenetrable cloak: the darts of the enemy shall not touch your soul. Your soul rests in Me.

"My beloved, it is My joy to protect you, because you will strive for Me. . ."

HYMN OF CHRISTIAN JOY

The following lyrical passage proclaims a Hymn of Christian Joy that forms a fitting summary of the preceding excerpts.

383. "My little daughter, serve Me with joy, give Me much joy—it bears witness to My Presence.

"I give to you, and you cannot offer Me anything better than My gifts; if you bring Me only pain and effort, you bring Me that which comes from yourself, and what have you done with the joy I sent you. . .?

"I am always in a joyous heart. Sadness reigns where I have not been welcomed. . .joy of soul, which the world does not always see, is the first of all your messages to rise to Heaven.

"Joy of living under authority, because authority should be a protection and a strength that directs you toward Me. When it is not so, I nevertheless use it thus in an obedient soul.

"Joy of obedience, because it expresses your love.

"Joy of purity and chastity which opens your eyes to the eternal light.

"Joy of poverty which makes you sharers in the divine capacity of *giving*.

"Joy of bodily suffering which sets the soul free.

"Joy of interior mortification which leads you ever deeper into the realms of the Spirit, where you pass from discovery to discovery until the day when you will meet Me face to face.

"Joy, joy, interior joy!

"My little daughter, you who have so easy a task, I desire you to convert everything into interior joy. Thus you glorify Me."

PERSONS IN THE GOSPELS

Certain persons from the Gospels are set forth as examples or warnings for souls: St. John the Evangelist, Judas, Simon of Cyrene, Veronica, St. Joseph and, most prominently, Mary, the Mother of God.

125. "It is not sufficient to say: 'My God, I have confidence in You!' You must make the interior act of freeing yourself from all anxiety, and rest on My Heart like the Apostle St. John at the Last Supper— yes, like St. John, the Beloved Apostle. I await this confidence from every soul..."

273. "My little daughter, beware of all avarice. It unconsciously introduces itself into a soul. It shuts the soul out from My Kingdom. Avarice is the cause of lying—of all crimes, of all denials, of all treason.

"The attachment to passing goods which one desires to possess and to hold, hates My Spirit and wishes to destroy It. Avarice is the work of death. Think of Judas. Watch and pray so as to fight it with a strength worthy of your name of Christian."

387. "Simon the Cyrenean is carrying My Cross without knowing that he is cooperating in the Redemption.

"There are many who by acts of spontaneous charity carry My Cross and who also cooperate in the Redemption without knowing it.

"And yet they do not know Me; but they are of My family; I recognize them as Mine.

"Just as the world recognizes you by this: 'If you have love one for another'—by the same sign do I also recognize you."

388. "Veronica received a magnificent reward—but do you know how much her act cost her in courage and heroic charity?

"I am not less generous today than then. The manifestation of My divine rewards awaits your heroic charity. . ."

416. "Simon the Cyrenean, without knowing it, carried the Cross of Redemption. He helped Me more than Veronica. Nevertheless he did not receive an immediate reward because there was less love in his help than in Veronica's action. You see, it is love that honors Me and that I reward.

"However Simon the Cyrenean did carry My Cross, and that will remain his for eternity. . . ."

444. "Simon was 'constrained' to carry My Cross. When I send you trials, I oblige you also to carry the crosses which you would not willingly have accepted of yourselves.

"It was a great glory for Simon the Cyrenean. It is also for your glory when I honor you with sufferings. Accept them all as coming from Me. And remember that all I say to you, as all I send you—it is always because I love you and wish you to be altogether Mine..."

445. "Veronica is a diamond on the Way of Sorrows. Little was needed to comfort Me, a compassion stronger than selfishness!

"The Way of Sorrows is still, throughout the centuries, the advance of humanity towards its eternity, and I am still with you in that advance...

"Now again, you see, it is easy to comfort Me: each time that generous love triumphs!

"It is love that makes reparation—it is love that leads to the folly of the Cross.

"Can I count on yours?..."

470. "Certainly, Christ's sufferings were sufficient to redeem you without any human cooperation.

"But God has ordained that My Mother should be Co-Redemptrix of the human race, and Mediatrix of all Graces.

"He willed that the Cyrenean should help Me to carry My Cross to show you that each one of you must join his share of efforts to Mine if you wish to benefit by the work of the Redemption...."

326. "Be kind—render your Sisters every possible service, but strive to do it without appearing to be useful or necessary. That is not good for souls, either for your own or for others, and it requires a purification; for, notice: neither My Father nor I act that way, nor do the Angels; never did the Blessed Virgin, or St. Joseph, or any of the Saints make

themselves appear necessary—on the contrary. The prayers of My Saints obtained miracles, and they loudly attributed them to others...."

9. "...I have given you My Mother to enlighten your way. Look at her, the Morning Star...."

188. "See, in the Cribs they place Me, not on My Mother's lap, but on the straw; because she did not keep Me for herself; she gave Me to the human race even before My birth...."

237. "Yes, I have made Myself so truly your Brother that I have willed that you should have the same Father as I, and that My Mother should become your Mother.

"Love does not keep for itself those whom it loves, it gives them away..."

427. "Never appear alone before the Most Holy Trinity, but always with Me who pray within you, and with My Mother. We have adopted you, and you have given Me your humanity: I wish to live again in you..."

37. "...You must simplify, reduce your necessities as My Mother did. You must make calm and wise decisions with a calm mind.

"The right order is to seek first, in all things, the Kingdom of God and His justice, and the rest shall be added unto you...."

207. "When I seem to you to be hidden very far away, seek Me in gentleness—gentleness towards

others, towards yourself, towards Me. Oh, if you knew
how gentle the Blessed Virgin is, and how happy
I am among the gentle—they delight Me. . .Where
gentleness reigns, there your Jesus smiles."

241. "I wish a gentle happiness to reign among you.
Strive to be gentle. Think of My Mother: do you not
then feel the sweetness of her smile in your soul?"

446. "My little daughter, I wish you daily to offer
a special prayer to My Mother for Superiors, all Superiors.

"There are too few who understand their responsibilities and correspond with them.

"Authority is sacred; it comes from God.

"It should be a protection for those confided to
it, imitating in their regard My Mother's way of acting: considerate and silent, maternal and remote,
invisible in its protection—making the same demands as God makes, and being itself a source of
grace for its children. . . ."

259. "It is when a soul forgives and is silent that
she most resembles My Mother."

365. "Where there is no injustice, there is not the
highest virtue, that which expiates and makes reparation. There may be other virtues, but not the one
which I practiced by preference in My apostolic life
and in My Passion, which My Mother practiced,
which I ask of souls who are dearest to Me, which
I expect of My Spouses.

"It is where injustice exists that you are called
to overcome evil by good."

469. "You do well to feel compassion for My Mother. You will never feel too much when you think of the Way of the Cross. She shared all My sufferings; she drank the bitter chalice to the dregs; with Me she worked your Redemption. You must adore rather than seek to understand this mystery of her cooperation:

"It is one of the Father's mercies..."

154. "Yes, you can console and thank My Mother; you can daily make reparation for the sufferings she endured, every time you imitate her.—Ask her to melt your heart into her own."

LITTLE PARABLES

"When I spoke to My disciples, I took advantage of what was happening around us: look in the Gospels. I have not changed." (No. 274). In the following "little parables" are found many of the same images used in the Gospels—the seed, light, water—as well as other striking images from more recent times.

7. "If you give Me nothing, I am not able to do the good which I leave to your initiative. Give Me the tiny seed of your sacrifices, of your efforts; I will make it fruitful. But give Me the seed...."

497. "Yes, you see the beautiful things that I make with the tiniest seeds...because they are surrendered to My action.

"What would I not make with acts of confidence, of faith, of hope, of charity, surrendered to My Omnipotence...?"

498. "Yes, be My little seed planted here in the

soil of Jerusalem, to produce here fruit in My Church—fruit and many other seeds according to My prodigality.

"Let Me act. But let your obedience be perfect; like the seed surrendered to My action.

"You know that the grain of wheat must die so that it may yield fruit."

249. "In difficult situations, whatever they may be, you can always be generous through striving to overcome evil by good. It is the interior effort that matters; it *is* for eternity, the visible result matters little; it is the interior effort which will produce fruit at harvest time...."

579. "When you are united in prosperity and peace, is your union sound?

"When you are united through trials, through the roughness of difficult characters, in spite of antipathies and sufferings, your union is like a strong plant that gives glory to God. Its roots bury themselves deeply in the hidden earth, through the rocky ground that impeded its growth. It will resist all storms.

"So must you strengthen each other and look to Heaven."

303. "What gives the fields and the woods, the valleys and the little hills their beauty?

"It is the light with which I inundate them.

"So it is with your soul; it is My grace that gives it all beauty; it is My grace that makes it attractive and lovable; it seizes every opportunity of introducing itself into your soul and of transforming it.

Multiply these opportunities. Do not tire of imploring My grace..."

481. "My Spirit diffuses Itself, gently, imperceptibly, without any noise. It has an irresistible gentleness and strength like the sun...When the sun invades the earth, who can resist it?

"And it animates everything. It is when you keep silent that My Spirit can work: you give it room."

559. "It is the sun that gives the earth its beauty and animates it.

"It is My grace that gives souls their beauty and that animates them.

"My Omnipotence is limited only by your liberty.

"It is with coal that I make diamonds.

"What would I not do with a soul, however black she might be, who would give herself to Me!"

628. "Each day you see the light change in color and the night return. It happens in a continual, imperceptible manner.

"Thus do I transform your souls, imperceptibly, gradually, without your being able to determine the moment when the change takes place!

"Thus do I change the circumstances in your lives to make them work together for the greater good of your soul—that is a mere game for divine power!

"And that same power can do nothing in your soul, without your acquiescence!"

308. "I am the Source from which the waters flow inexhaustibly, with abundance. But you must *come* to the Source to drink. Come, all of you! Do not stop

by the way: life eternal is near you: accept it!"

517. "In difficulty, seek your comfort in Me alone. Ask to obtain the fruit of the trial without delay, so that it may cease.

"I am the Source. Come to the Source. It is inexhaustible. . . ."

518. "I am the Source: come and draw from it!

"I will give you what you need at every moment: strength, joy, courage, meekness, patience, charity, wisdom. . . At every moment. But come. . . I am your life. . . ."

43. "Just as storms are necessary in nature, so are they necessary in every living soul.

"Do not lose your serenity on account of those who are being tried. Pray for them; offer the sufferings of My Passion and some acts of self-denial, some self-imposed sufferings for them."

164. "No, there is not a single superfluous suffering in your life. Your heart must be rent that My grace may penetrate it; otherwise you remain as a closed garden within your own feelings, your own thoughts, your horizon.

"Your horizon must be rent, so that you may catch a glimpse of the destiny to which you are called. Your destiny is so great that according to nature, you could not of yourselves imagine it. Your heart must be rent that My grace may penetrate and transform it."

235. "A little effort and pain, then such a great

reward—and already here below the reward of seeing love, generosity, and the Faith spread irresistibly, like a spot of oil...."

196. "I send you sparks of joy; it depends on you to enkindle it or to let it burn out like a lamp without oil. But it is not in your power to repress the revolts of nature; there are souls who always have to struggle. Pray for rebellious hearts whom the Holy Spirit alone can pacify...."

506. "If you wish to love Me, think of Me.

"In order to think of Me, love Me.

"Think of what you know about Me: your love will grow—and it is love that will give you a deeper knowledge, new thoughts.

"Love is the fireplace, the furnace; thought, the spark..."

"And what is it that feeds the fire?"

"Is it not you, My victim...?"

584. "My little daughter, your thoughts are the rudder of your little boat.

"It is I who guide your little boat by the movement of the wind and the waves, but it is also you who guide it, if your rudder follows My suggestions.

"Let your thoughts remain fixed on Me...."

625. "My little daughter, to hit the target, good marksmen aim above it—then they hit it. Do you understand?

"To practice a virtue, do not be afraid of exaggerating that virtue—to attain to the love of the Cross, you must know the folly of the Cross."

557. "...Just as you train yourselves in hiking for mountain-climbing, in developing skills in the fine arts, and in perfecting yourselves in your professions, so can you train yourselves in generosity in the service of God. Many souls deprive themselves of many graces because they refuse to make efforts which seem impossible to them, which are only offered to the generosity of their initiative. They remain in mediocrity, ignorant of the reserves of energy and of love hidden in their soul. Because they do not exhaust all their possibilities, they also do not know how much I can help them...."

213. "As a rule, to do a little more than is required is to offer Me the perfume with the flower. This little extra effort, being voluntary, can only be an expression of love; it is more precious than all the rest; and usually it is neither seen nor known by anyone; it is for Me alone that it is done: it is the perfume of the flower..."

577. "...The good Spirit, the Holy Spirit is like a breath of joy that carries everything along on its way. He is contagious. By His very nature He diffuses His joy as a rose gives its perfume. Give way to Him!..."

231. "You are nothing—a nonentity.
"Be pure like a drop of dew, that My Face may be reflected in you.
"It is because you are nothing that I can take possession of you, substitute Myself for you...."

550. "You are in God, in His Power, as leaves abandoned to a breath of wind.

"And I have made Myself
"dependent on you, I your God...."

556. "Remain fixed in Me—like the little magne-
tized needle of the compass. The creatures who led
you to Me no longer exist for you, since you have
met Me. They exist *in Me*. And your gratitude to
them will be your fidelity in following Me...."

466. "When you sweep you see the frightened
spiders, instead of running along the ground, struggle to climb the highest walls.

"Imitate them; keep your soul on the heights,
above the blows of life's broom, in the realms not
reached by human pettinesses; in My Kingdom..."

570. "When a soul is threatened by dangers of
which she is not aware, I cover her with a cloak
that she may be shielded from the malice of the
wicked: this cloak that I give her is *simplicity*."

201. "It is you yourselves who weave your own
happiness. I have given you the threads, and it is
for you to weave the design of your happiness, hour
by hour. Contemplation is indispensable to this work,
because you can reproduce only those designs with
which you have impregnated yourselves by contemplating them.

"Silence is indispensable to this work.

"And because it is necessary to choose that which
is essential, to choose it incessantly, letting go of
all that is superfluous, poverty is indispensable to
this work.

"Obedience will give the measure of your skill,

and it is love that will give to this work its coloring,
its life, and its beauty..."

THE HEART OF JESUS

*"God so loved the world, as to give His only begotten
Son." (John 3:16). "As the Father has loved Me, also
I have loved you..." (John 15:9). The whole of the
life of Jesus as portrayed in the Gospels is a revelation of the love of God for His creatures. This Love
is embodied in His Heart. The following Notes illustrate the unique place each person holds in the Heart
of Jesus, the response He looks for in the lives of
His followers, and the resulting union of hearts.*

GOD'S UNIQUE LOVE FOR EACH PERSON

247. "...I wish each soul to understand that she
has her special place in My Heart which awaits her;
that her love is necessary to Me; and her cooperation necessary—that I need to see her happy and
perfect—because I have loved her even to dying on
the Cross for her—yes, each soul...."

152. "Fervent souls console Me for the lukewarm-
ness, for the forgetfulness of sinners. But they do
not take the place of the souls I desire; each one
has her place in My Heart, each one is loved for
something unique that I have given her, and I cannot be consoled for their loss while there is hope
of their repentance. The few sheep do not compen-
sate Me for the hundredth that has strayed. Each
soul is a matchless treasure to Me."

377. "Your friend? She is as precious to Me as
a pearl, very precious. She has a chosen place in
My Heart, and she will attain to it. My Mother has

a special love for her."

GOD'S DESIRE TO GIVE HIS LOVE

47. "...Your real cloister, without boundaries, is My Heart; it is your refuge and your cradle. It is always open; it is always awaiting you. It will give you joy, strength, meekness, love. For I wish you to be joyous and strong, irresistibly loving—and very meek."

54. "I wish you to be entirely Mine. You are so miserable! You have such need of Me! I will shelter you in the secret places of My Heart; you are My tiny child! Together we will accomplish some good...."

134. "It is not merely that you may pray there that I wish to bury you in My Heart; it is that you may learn there what love is—how far love leads.

"You would like to see Me loved by all men? In the measure in which you love Me, you will contribute to that, because love is an irresistible current, more powerful than the weight of sin.

"A single soul, however little she may be, possessed by love, can draw a multitude...."

157. "At the least sign of repentance, My Heart is aflame with joy, and I wait with *inexpressible* love for the sinner to turn towards Me...."

177. "At every absolution from the priest I blot out your sins, and blot them out again, and I press you to My Heart because you are Mine; I bought you at the price of My Blood, the Blood of God...."

THE RESPONSE GOD SEEKS

4. "Kindness...Indulgence...Keep your soul free and transparent, above the troubles, cares, and misunderstandings which the cloister produces...

"Teach, only by example. Silence, silence in the Heart of your God."

14. "...Bury yourself in My Heart, and let Me act; then I shall use you. I shall use you to bring many Protestants back to the Church, and in a way beyond all that you can imagine, because I work as God. It is as God that I keep My promises: it is as God that I am pleased to respond to humble confidence...."

114. "...Let Me act; you are not competent to do anything; it is not your province. Your place is in My Heart where I wish you to be buried, praying unceasingly for souls; and I will work...."

147. "Your corporal penances please Me, however small they may be, in the measure in which they help you to master, together with your body, your mind, your imagination, your memory, your will, in order to give them to Me, to place them in My Heart, where they will find all they need...."

177. "Remain in My Heart, and I will teach you what Love is. Do you not desire to live a little as I lived?..."

243. "Believe what I tell you; your confidence consoles Me for the little confidence given Me by so many others who, nevertheless, are of My family.

My heart was pierced by the lance—it is still often pierced by the lack of understanding on the part of those who only half listen to Me...."

245. "...You remain near Me, but your mind is saturated with mere nothings! It is as if you fell asleep at My Feet while My Heart was calling you.

"I want you to be awake and listening...."

280. "...I do not enforce My wishes—I hardly express clearly My desires for additional acts of generosity...Those who love guess each others' desires: so it is between Me and the soul that loves Me.

"The most touching joy is given Me when a soul foresees what I desire of her, even before I have asked it of her...My heart is reflected in hers...

"Souls must come to Me of themselves."

289. "There are sacrifices which I desire, but for which I do not ask—so as to leave to souls the joy of offering them to Me of themselves. These souls are hidden in the depths of My Heart, they embrace its suggestions...

"My Mother has communicated something of her love to them...."

295. "My little daughter, be full of happiness, so that others imitating you may speed toward Heaven that *thanks* which My Heart loves to reward magnificently..."

354. "Obedience is a state of the soul, a permanent state which makes the soul cling perseveringly to the will of God, and immediately to the manifold

opportunities which she is given to submit her own will to that of others. Obedience, My little daughter, is something very deep and very powerful, yes, even irresistible, with the Heart of God...."

374. "A tiny sin of no importance, but wilfully committed, causes Me immense pain and prepares you for the worst acts of cowardice. You know it, but do you know as clearly that a tiny pain, a mere nothing, but *wilfully* done to one of your Sisters, wounds My Heart, and prepares you for a denial of Love...."

421. "I washed My disciples' feet and more than that: look at the Cross. Then do you not believe that I am able to come to your help now?

"Have I not proved the love of My Heart enough for you to believe in it?..."

482. "You have a good deal of pride, much more than you realize. I recommend as a remedy this prayer that I have such joy in granting: 'Jesus, meek and humble of Heart, make my heart like unto Thine.'

"Say it incessantly, from the moment you awaken, to protect yourself and to make reparation for the faults your pride has caused."

483. "...The soul that makes reparation gives Me two joys: she re-establishes order—and above all: she erases from My Heart the pain caused by the unfaithful soul, because by making reparation she arouses repentance—and nothing consoles Me so much as a repentant soul. She becomes My beloved..."

613. ". . .The interior union of hearts that love one another and of wills that wish the good of others—that is your strength, an invincible power even over the Heart of God. . . ."

THE UNION OF HEARTS

65. "Since you love Me, you will also have your hands, feet, and heart pierced, *if you will allow it.* Your heart, by being separated from all creatures; your hands, by dedicating them to work that does not please you; your feet will not go where they would like to walk. But it will not be to a cross that you will be voluntarily nailed; you will be riveted to My Heart so that nothing may again separate you from Me. And if you will consent to it with love, I will increase your love and I will fill your whole being.

"Let it be done to you."

246. "It was because I neither defended Myself nor complained during My Passion that they insulted and abused Me beyond all measure.

"If you do not complain—if you do not let your weariness be guessed—if you do not defend yourself and if you allow yourself to be stripped, they will abuse your good will—but you will be imitating Me. It is thus that I shall be able to live again in you, thus and in no other way.

"It is thus that I who live in you will Myself carry you further in My Heart, towards your God."

370. ". . .And the most favored souls? Oh, there are many! They are those whom I call to join Me in the Apostolate of My Eucharistic Life. They are

the richest in grace because I give them the strength they need to respond to what I ask of them. And it is as if I hide them in the deepest depths of My Heart: their life is all in Me."

501. "My beloved, I wish to fill you with joy! Humiliations, contempt, being forgotten by other creatures, these are the joys that I will give you. Because each pain that comes from creatures will make you enter more deeply into My Heart, into My Heart that calls you, into My Heart that awaits you. . . ."

607. ". . . Do you understand that if all your actions fall into My Heart to rejoice it and to bury themselves there, I can use them through time and space according to the desires of My Heart?"

520. "We are alone, face to face.

"Soon death will place you before Me, alone, face to face."

"My Lord Jesus, what will become of me, I who am nothing but sin?"

"It is My Heart that awaits you. . . ."

The extent of the love and concern of God for each individual is beautifully set forth in the following Note which summarizes His action in the life of Sister Mary of the Holy Trinity. A similar summary could be written of the life of every person if only each would allow it, for: "Formerly I spoke in parables. In the secret intimacy of the soul, I speak softly, for it is necessary that a soul should come to Me of herself." (No. 284).

HYMN OF LOVE

335. "Because I love you, I have simplified your life: I have given you no other responsibility than your daily fidelity.

"Because I love you I have given you bad health in order that from the beginning of your life you might feel your dependence on Me—in order that you might receive strength every day from Me, and not from your body.

"Because I love you I wanted you to be poor, altogether poor, so that I alone would be your life.

"Because I love you I put you on the road that leads to My Church.

"I gave you the gift of Faith.

"Because I love you I put fervent souls in your path who have prayed much for you.

"Because I love you I have given you here on earth the prayers of a saint who has guarded your vocation and has strengthened it.

"Because I love you, I have given you here on earth a spiritual Father.

"Because I love you I have confided you since your birth to the Virgin Mary, your Mother.

"Because I love you I have given you a desire for penance and the strength to do penance.

"Because I love you I have given you the five Vows which bind you to Me.

"Because I love you, I died for you on the Cross.

"What will you give Me?..."

5

PRAYERS OF SISTER MARY OF THE TRINITY

A FAVORITE PRAYER OF SISTER MARY OF THE TRINITY

The following is a fourth-century Syriac prayer for inner peace and grace which Sister Mary found and liked so much that she copied it (in French) on a slip of paper that was eventually given to Raphael Brown. This is his translation, reproducing the Sister's punctuation, capitalization, underlining and line lengths.

May your <u>peace</u>, Lord, and your
tranquility, your charity and your grace,
the mercy of your divinity be
with us and among us, all the
days of our life, now, at
all times, and even for centuries
on centuries — Amen

The theme of inner tranquility as essential for the spiritual life is of course basic, especially in the Christian East. It is summed up in this saying of St. Isaac.

"In meekness and tranquility, simplify your soul."

OFFERING TO THE HOLY TRINITY

This undated prayer appears in the Sister's handwriting among the illustrations in Father Duboin's book. This translation retains the division of the lines in the original. We do not have the final word(s).

O Father, who are God, here I hold out my hands
to accept sufferings and to receive them as
a gift from You: may Your Reign come!

O Son, who are God, here I raise my hands
to offer my sufferings as a sacrifice through
You: may Your Reign come!

O Holy Spirit, who are God, here I raise
my hands to offer my sufferings as
a sacrifice through You: may Your Reign come!

O Holy Trinity, through Jesus, with Jesus and
    in Jesus,
may my sufferings give You all honor and
glory! So be it.

Grant me, Lord, to enter fully into this vocation
of suffering: make me worthy of suffering!
You have given me a weak and frail body.
O Father, here I am to fulfill Your Holy [Will].

All the following prayers are taken from The Spiritual
Legacy of Sister Mary of the Holy Trinity.

MORNING OFFERING

My Lord Jesus, here is my tongue that You may
watch over it; that it may not utter more than
pleases You; and that my silence may speak to You.

Here are my ears that they may listen only to the
voice of duty, and to Your voice, O Jesus!

Here are my eyes that they may not cease to behold You in every face and in every work.

Here are my hands and my feet that You may

make them agile, that You may rivet them to Your service alone, to the execution of Your desires.

Here are my thoughts that Your Light may possess them.

Here is my heart that Your Love, O Jesus, may reign and rest in it!

*   *   *

"Renew this offering every morning, at every Holy Communion.

"And I give you, My little daughter, I give you *today*."   (Page 342)

PRAYERS TO FULFILL GOD'S WILL

My Lord, *yes*, to all You desire,
with Your help,
with all my will,
with all my initiative,
with all my soul,
from now on.   (No. 536)

My Lord Jesus,
if You wish that I should glorify You in this way,
    may You be praised!
If You wish that I should glorify You in another way,
    may You be praised!
It is Your will that I desire.   (No. 540)

My God, my God,
All that You have given me, take it;
take *all* that I have!   (No. 335)

My Lord Jesus, yes, yes, yes!   (No. 518)

My Lord Jesus, what can I do?
I long to have a thousand lives
so as to consecrate them all to You
and to begin again what I have so badly done!
                                                    (No. 524)

My Lord Jesus,
grant that before I die,
I may at least have served You for one day as
   You desire;
without any neglect—any breach of silence, or
   regularity—
with no want of generosity, of joy,
   or of love towards all. Amen.   (No. 343)

My Lord Jesus,
my wandering thoughts escape me...
Take them, take them, take them forever!
Fill them with Yourself,
that they may no longer think of anything but You—
fix them on Yourself as in their eternity—
And grant that all Your desires for Your little
   creature
may be accomplished,
one after the other, calmly and fully!   (No. 316)

My Lord Jesus,
I came that You might give me
what I wanted to ask of You—
then I stayed in order to love You better, serve You
   better,
to thank You—
even though You have not granted me the
   conversions I asked for.

And now can I have a single desire
that is not Yours...?
You know it, You know it so well...   (No. 339)

PRAYERS TO GROW IN LOVE

Oh, my God, my God, my God!
I only ask You for love,
to love You as You desire to be loved.
Break my heart;
give me Your love.   (No. 20)

My God, it is You who give all;
deign to teach me how to love You!   (No. 359)

Oh, my God, my God, I desire You alone!
You know it!   (No. 48)

My Lord Jesus,
give me the necessary dispositions
   for receiving Your gifts!   (No. 169)

PRAYERS FOR UNITY

My God, You are a Spirit.
You are not accepted among us if we do not love
   one another.
Give us the grace to love one another!
Give us the grace to receive You!
Grant that we may love one another.   (No. 50)

My Lord Jesus,
grant that there may no longer be a single second in
my life, a single fiber of my heart that does not
foster the accomplishment of Your will in me and
in those around me, my Lord Jesus...   (No. 144)

Oh, my Lord Jesus, [I desire]
only Your love and Your grace
and that You may keep me in this very simple life,
where without any other responsibility
than my fidelity at every moment,
I can live with You in secret—
and strive with all my being
for that union of feelings and actions
which must *unite* all Christians in You,
my Lord Jesus!   (No. 235)

I have done no good—
and I have sinned.
But now I feel, I *know,* O my God,
that You will bring to pass,
beyond all that I can imagine,
my immense desires for union
among souls of goodwill for Your glory!
I will intercede until the end of the world.
It will be You who will work.
Here I am, ready, awaiting Your call,
as Your crusader, watching. . .   (No. 541)

My Lord Jesus,
it is then that I shall begin to do good on earth,
because it is *You* who will send me!   (No. 520)

PRAYERS TO THE BLESSED VIRGIN MARY

Holy Virgin Mary! Oh, my Mother,
You took part in the Passion!
You who are the Co-redemptrix,
You who are the Mediatrix of all Graces,
teach me to live this Lent as Jesus desires—
this Lent may be the last in this poor life

that has so offended God.
Teach me to make reparation for my faults
and for those I have caused others to commit—
to take my part in the whole work of Reparation.
(No. 317)

My Mother, my sweet Mother,
entrust this poor life to Jesus,
that henceforth He may wholly fill it—
and that He may do with it what He wills!
Teach me, O Mother of Christ! to give Him all.
(No. 27)

PRAYERS FOR THE GRACE OF SUFFERING

My God, change my hard heart
into a resemblance of Your gentleness and humility!
Deign to give me sorrow for my sins.
Give me tears to weep over Your Passion,
grant that I may understand it better!   (No. 459)

My God, You know all:
My desire to expiate,
to make reparation, to love You,
to glorify You by suffering. . .
You are silent, my God,
but I feel in Your silence that You accept it
and that You will fulfill it. . .   (No. 554)

It is for martyrdom I ask, my God!
My life brings You nothing—
Let me die for You, in obedience.   (No. 542)

PRAYER FOR CONVERSIONS

My Lord Jesus, You are the Truth.
The Truth is worth more than all riches.
There is no sacrifice too great in order to find You.
Make them find You,
You and Your Church,
and grant that I may carry a little of their Cross,
so that they may not be crushed by it.   (No. 253)

OFFERING OF THE NEW YEAR

My Lord Jesus, this new year is for You.
Give me the grace
not to waste a single moment of it.
Give me the dispositions that You desire
so that You may be able
unceasingly to bestow on me
Your love and Your grace.   (No. 185)

PROMISE OF FAITHFULNESS

My God, *today* I begin again my poor life. . .
I will have no thought for anything but You
    and the duty of my state;
for You who have waited so long for me—
and how I have wasted Your gifts, wasted
    precious time!   (No. 27)

6

Epilogue and Bibliography
FRANCISCAN CONNECTIONS
by Raphael Brown

In this discursive epilogue I shall outline for the record some background data about the origin and development of the several French and English editions of the Notebooks and life of Sister Mary of the Trinity, with brief biographical sketches of their editors, translators and authors, plus some relevant information which I have received in correspondence from the two friar editors, from the Poor Clares in Jerusalem, England, Switzerland and Rockford, and from a lifelong friend of the Sister, the Swiss Dr. Lydia von Auw.

Thus it becomes evident that a fairly complex network of "Franciscan connections" has been involved in the backdrop and evolution of this book, a network in which are interwoven all three branches of the family of St. Francis: First Order Fathers and Brothers, Second Order cloistered contemplative Poor Clare nuns, and Third Order—now called Secular Franciscan Order—lay persons. Geographically the network extends from Switzerland to Italy, the Holy Land, France, Belgium, England and the United States, with strife-torn South Africa on the distant horizon. And in addition to the Franciscan family there are also two Cistercian links. It is our earnest belief and hope that all this information will not only be of real interest but may also serve to inspire and unite the greater spiritual family of Sisters and friends of Sister Mary of the Trinity.

A brief biographical sketch of her spiritual director in Jerusalem in the years 1938 - 1942, Father Silvère van den Broek, O.F.M. (1889 - 1949), will be found on page 20 of *The Spiritual Legacy*. Before leaving the Holy Land in 1946, he published the first edition of the Notes of Sister Mary of the Trinity and her account of her "Conversion and Vocation"; this was published in Beirut, Lebanon, in 1943, with favorable preliminary letters from Ignatius Gabriel Cardinal Tappouni and Monsignor Luigi Barlassini, Latin Patriarch of Jerusalem. Soon after Father Silvère's return to Belgium, a second French edition was published by the Imprimerie Saint François in Malines.

Meanwhile, in 1946 I had come across an article on Sister Mary of the Trinity, with passages from her Notes, in the Italian Franciscan magazine, *Terra Santa*. I then obtained and read the Beirut book. On December 14, 1946, I wrote to Sister Mary of the Trinity's Father confessor (without knowing his name) in care of St. Saviour's Friary in Jerusalem, thanking him for publishing the book which, I hoped, would perhaps do as much good in souls as the Little Flower's *Story of a Soul,* and I offered to help in having it translated and published in English.

Father Silvère replied from Malines on January 14, 1947, saying that though he was busy hearing confessions in a score of convents, he was nevertheless working on a biography of the Sister, and that he had heard from the nuns in Jerusalem that the

Poor Clares of Bullingham in England were also interested in the translating. So he judiciously decided that they would do the Notes and I should do the rest, with both translators conferring and submitting their texts for his revision.

Thus I began a fruitful correspondence, collaboration and friendship with Sister Mary Gabriel which extended until her death in 1966 at the age of ninety-one. She was indeed a remarkably gifted nun. A convert from the Church of England, she had a late vocation, becoming a Poor Clare only in her fifties. Sister (later Abbess) Mary Fidelis, who was with her as a novice, wrote me: "We were great friends, so I shared a lot in her thoughts, in the books she translated. Sister was a lovely soul, very artistic, in fact an artist to her fingertips." Mother Mary Michael, Abbess in 1966, noted that "dear Sister Gabriel's mental energy was always very great." Her translating "gave her great pleasure, and I am sure it was partially the reason why her mind kept so clear to the end." She was also active in preparing leaflets and a selection of excerpts from the Notes (which is included in this present book).

In fact, after completing work on Sister Mary of the Trinity's book and arranging for its publication by Mercier Press, Sister Mary Gabriel, despite a cataract in 1952, worked with me for another ten years on a translation of all seven French volumes of *Lui et moi* (*He and I*) by the secular Franciscan Gabrielle Bossis (d. 1950). Unfortunately our lengthy labor of love was never published because we were unable to find a British or American publisher who would accept the terms of the Editions Beauchesne in Paris. But in 1969 an excellent translation of the first two

volumes by Evelyn M. Brown (no relation to myself)
was brought out by the Editions Paulines in Sher-
brooke, Canada.

After several refusals (though far fewer than the
fifteen endured by my translation of Felix Timmermans' *The Perfect Joy of St. Francis*), *The Spiritual
Legacy of Sister Mary of the Holy Trinity*, consisting
principally of the Sister's Notes and her account of
her "Conversion and Vocation," was accepted in 1949
by Newman Press in Westminster, Maryland under
John J. McHale. To promote its distribution I alerted
all the Poor Clare communities in the United States
and submitted selections of excerpts on various topics
to several magazines. Over a dozen reviews welcomed
and praised the book. In 1981 *The Spiritual Legacy*
was republished by TAN Books and Publishers, Inc.
in cooperation with the Poor Clares of Rockford,
Illinois. Between 1981 and 1987 the TAN edition
sold 12,000 copies. Sales in France were over 8,000,
plus 1,000 in Switzerland and 600 in French Canada.
Translations into German, Italian, and Flemish also
appeared.

In 1971 Father Bartholomew Gottemoller, o.c.s.o.,
of the Cistercian Abbey of the Holy Trinity at Hunts-
ville, Utah, compiled a hundred-page book of *Words
of Love Spoken by Our Lord to Three Twentieth-
Century Victim Souls: Sister Josefa Menendez, Sister Mary of the Trinity, and Sister Consolata Betrone;*
this was first printed by his abbey in 1971 and then
published in 1985 by TAN Books and Publishers.
(Incidentally, TAN also publishes Sister Josefa's *The
Way of Divine Love* and sells Sister Consolata's *Jesus
Appeals to the World*.) After an Introduction on the
three nuns, Father Bartholomew groups brief yet

striking excerpts from their writings under thirty-four subject sections.

Also in 1985 Alba House published *Revelations of Women Mystics from the Middle Ages to Modern Times,* by Dr. Jose de Vinck, to whom we are indebted for the excellent five-volume translation of *The Works of Bonaventure* (St. Anthony Guild Press). Among the *Revelations* is a chapter (pages 129-147) on and by Louisa Jaques (Sister Mary of the Trinity).

On a deeply moving pilgrimage to the Holy Land in 1960, by special permission I was able to visit the cemetery of the Poor Clares outside Jerusalem with the Franciscan Custody's forceful American Father Patrick Coyle. Every Christmas the nuns and I exchange letters. They report that visits to the cemetery are increasing over the years. They also correspond several times a year with their Sister's beloved sister, Alice, who resides with her husband in the United States and who prays with and for them.

Apart from still having no heat in the bitter-cold winters, the main problem of the nearly twenty nuns at the Jerusalem Poor Clare monastery remains that of new vocations, though one would expect that more than enough candidates would come to such a uniquely hallowed site from the over twenty Poor Clare communities in France. As they write, "Our monastery has the good fortune of having on the east not buildings but the woods of Jerusalem and the valleys [of the Judean desert]. We can always gaze at the sites of the Gospels: Bethphage by the Mount of Olives, Bethany, and the mountains of Moab in the distance. We love to pray facing those places which forever sing of Jesus."

Among their friends and helpers of the Franciscan Custody, they have especially mentioned our own friend over the past forty years, Brother Roger Petras from the Franciscan Monastery of the Holy Land in Washington, who has served as custodian of the lovely little Shepherds' Field Chapel near Bethlehem and as one of the Discretes of the Custody. The Sisters were deeply inspired by the visit on September 6, 1979, of our Californian Minister General John Vaughn: "We were quite struck by his serenity, his simplicity, his humility...it was an immense grace we could never forget!"

The promises of Jesus to Sister Mary of the Trinity that the Poor Clares would one day return to Switzerland were fulfilled over twenty years later when in 1964 some of the nuns from the revived Evian community founded a convent near Geneva (see Notes 53, 88, 97, 114, 276).

On January 12, 1976, the five Poor Clares of Geneva moved to Jongny near Vevey at the eastern end of Lake Geneva, where three more soon joined them. Six of the eight Sisters are French, one is Belgian, and one Swiss. There are three novices. The community expects soon to become independent.

The Poor Clares were providentially invited to Vevey, where St. Colette's foundation had resided for over a century (from 1424 to 1536), by the trustees of a beautiful twenty-acre estate named *La Grant Part* after an old motto, *En petit lieu à Dieu grand part*—"In a small place a great share for God." (That "small place" reminds us of St. Francis' beloved "Little Portion," the "Portiuncola" Chapel where he and later St. Clare founded their Orders.) This wooded estate on the gentle slopes of Mont Pelerin north of Vevey, overlooking one of the most beautiful lakes in the world, had been deeded along with its mansion by Mademoiselle Yvonne Guyot on her death in 1971, to be preserved by a board of trustees "as a spiritual reservation in a natural reservation . . .open to all believers."

So the Poor Clares undertook to maintain (rent free) the mansion and adjacent grounds (while a farmer cultivated the rest of the estate) and to make this "small place" one in which God would have "a great share," by living and giving witness to the spiritual experience and values of Franciscan joy in poverty, simplicity, contemplative prayer and silence. Thus they seek to follow a religious way of life that will "sing of God's creation, as Francis did." The nuns labor at various crafts in voluntary material insecurity, while welcoming groups of children or adults who wish to spend a prayerful day in nature, without charge but with the contribution of voluntary maintenance work.

I am especially glad to be able to share this encouraging report on the new Poor Clare community near Vevey because I spent several happy years there as a schoolboy in the 1920's. In fact, my intense interest in the life and writings of Sister Mary of the Trinity stems from *four* basic links with my own life and work.

First, of course, is the Franciscan family connection. In 1942, with my good wife Gertrude and as a fruit of her prayers, I returned to the Church—in order to belong with her (a former Lutheran) to the spiritual family of St. Francis in his Third Order, now known as the Secular Franciscan Order.

Second, my love for Franciscanism and the Holy Land was stimulated by our devotion to "a St. Francis of our times," Good Father Frederic Janssoone (1838-1916), a Flemish-French friar who had served in Jerusalem before spending his last years in French Canada. On his beautiful life, see *An Apostle of Two Worlds* by the late Father Romain Légáre, O.F.M., which I translated for his Cause of Beatification (Editions Bon Père Frédéric, Trois Rivières, Québec, Canada, 1958). Incidentally, that book's Foreword was written by a friend and colleague of Father Silvère in Jerusalem: Father Paschal Kinsel, O.F.M., Commissary of the Holy Land at the famous Franciscan Monastery in Washington, D.C., which was founded in 1898 by Father Frederic's close friend, Father Godfrey Schilling, O.F.M. (d. 1934).

Again just for the record, to fill in further links of a striking chain of Franciscan connections, back in Belgium Father Silvère was also a friend of Father Maximin Piette, O.F.M. (d. 1948), who revised with me against the Flemish text my translation of Felix Timmermans' popular fictional life of St. Francis which I retitled *The Perfect Joy of St. Francis* (Image Books). Moreover, Father Piette's three French volumes on the life and letters of Padre Junipero Serra made an important contribution around 1950 to the Cause for Beatification of that famous founder of California's Franciscan missions by making available to the European and Roman public an extensive body of documentation on that saintly Majorcan priest whose 200th anniversary was celebrated in 1984/85. In 1985 the Holy See formally declared "Venerable" both Father Serra and Father Frederic.

Third, the French-Swiss background of our Poor Clare of Jerusalem was as meaningful to me as her Franciscan vocation and years in the Holy Land be-cause, as mentioned above, as a teenager I had spent most of the 1920's at two boarding schools on the lovely shores of Lake Geneva, first at Vevey and then near Morges, west of Lausanne, and Louisa Jaques had lived in that region in those years. In fact her sister Alice kindly wrote me a detailed description of the placid little town of Morges at that time.

And through the Sister's book I came to know and count among my best friends her lifelong friend Dr. Lydia von Auw, who lived in Morges around 1920 and has retired there in recent years after serving as a pastor of the Swiss Reformed Church. I had the pleasure of visiting her in Switzerland in 1962, and we exchange several letters each year. She has loaned me helpful books and sent me copies of her books and articles. Another striking Franciscan con-nection: she has made a lifelong study of the great medieval Franciscan spiritual leader Angelo Clareno (d. 1337), and has recently published a scholarly edi-tion of his letters and a thorough study of his life and spirituality. She gladly supplied information and correspondence from her friend Louisa to Fathers Silvère van den Broek and Alain Duboin for their books.

Some years ago the Poor Clares of Jerusalem in-formed me that Father Duboin was working on a new edition of the Notes of Sister Mary of the Trinity, and Dr. Lydia von Auw urged him to send me one of the first copies in 1979. I was delighted to find in his *Qu'un même amour nour rassemble* the rich new materials about her life and spirituality which he first made available and which we are now publishing in this present volume.

Father Alain-Marie Duboin was born in Geneva in 1915, joined the Friars Minor in 1943, and was ordained in 1949. In Switzerland the Capuchin Franciscans are far more numerous than the Order of Friars Minor, who have only a small Custody with 25 priests and brothers. After studies in Fribourg and Metz, Father Duboin labored at the friary in Fribourg from 1950 to 1970, serving after 1960 in a seminary for late vocations (which dissolved in 1970). He spent the next ten years in "a little paradise," the Custody's novitiate on a lovely tiny island in the Rhine River near the Lake of Constanz: St. Othmar im Werd, site of the tomb of that eighth-century abbot of the famous Abbey of Sankt Gallen. The island is within sight of the picturesque Swiss village of Stein-am-Rhein with its beautifully painted house facades. It was on this island that Father Duboin wrote and edited his book on Sister Mary of the Trinity and arranged to have a German translation published in Stein-am-Rhein by Christiana Verlag.

From 1980 until his untimely death on July 25, 1982, he ministered again in Fribourg, "the Swiss Rome," with its large Catholic university and seminaries. In some of his letters he deplored "the critical, anti-Roman spirit of a good part of the clergy" who were under the influence of Hans Küng, commenting that "the clerics bear a great responsibility in the decay of faith among believers."

The fourth factor in my response to the message of the Notes of Sister Mary of the Trinity was that such writings in which Jesus seems to speak directly

to us, as in many passages in the second half of
The Imitation of Christ, played a crucial role in
bringing me back to the Church in my search for
the purest and loftiest works of mystical literature,
as well as the finest examples of great lives lived
for God. As I wormed my way through one book after
another in my thirty years as a bookworm-employee
of the rich Library of Congress, I discovered a score
of such books. (Several have been republished by
TAN Books). Surely someone who takes one of those
books as spiritual reading will not only "accept" the
Lord Jesus—and His Church—but will also strive
daily to walk and talk with and obey and serve Him.

Now a few concluding lines about the recent gen-
esis of this book. We owe its publication (as well
as the 1981 TAN Books reprinting of *The Spiritual
Legacy of Sister Mary of the Holy Trinity*) to the fervent and practical initiative of Mother Mary Dorothy of the Holy Spirit, Abbess of the Colettine Poor
Clares of Corpus Christi Monastery in Rockford, Illinois, approximately 90 miles west of Chicago. Born
in 1939, she entered the community in 1959 and
found that since 1950 the nuns had been attracted
to the writings of their Sister in Jerusalem, "feeling an affinity to one of their own," whose "joys and
sorrows, victories and struggles were of the same
weave and texture as our own. Some of the most
refreshing hours of recreation in our small novitiate group sprang from the insights and inspirations
of Sister Mary of the Trinity. She quickly became
our elder sister instructing us in the spiritual life
and showing us how to satisfy the longings of Jesus'
Divine Heart by striving to let each hour unite us
more closely to Him. Her attraction and spiritual

friendship have deepened through the years. . ."

In 1978 Sister Dorothy was elected abbess by her community. "In recent times," she writes, "we asked ourselves what we could give to those interested in our form of life, especially those who wanted to know more about its spirituality. We turned to Sister Mary of the Trinity, feeling confident that she would be the perfect instructor. Her gentle person and strong character would be a bright light for those wishing to follow the way of our holy mother St. Clare. And for those not called, she would enrich their interior life. Even now our renewed interest in her and the discovery of the new French edition of her works and added biographical information have brought many blessings to our community."

On November 6, 1983, the *Chicago Tribune Magazine* published a well-written article by Robert McClory, with eight photos by Karen Engstrom, entitled "Hidden Goodness: Rockford's Poor Clares— The World Is Their Cloister," which I found so enlightening and relevant that I persuaded Mother Dorothy and TAN's publisher, Thomas Nelson, to reprint it as a fitting Appendix to this book. It provides a vivid illustration in word and picture of the life and spirituality of modern American Clares who, in joyful faithfulness and loving prayerfulness, live the spirit and example of Saints Clare and Colette and their Sister Mary of the Trinity, as do the nearly 18,000 Poor Clare nuns in 786 monasteries throughout the world (of which 27 are in the United States).

For readers wishing to know more about the life and spirituality of the Poor Clares, I recommend these basic works: *Francis and Clare, The Complete Works,* edited by Regis Armstrong, O.F.M. Cap., and

Ignatius Brady, O.F.M. (New York, Paulist Press, 1982); *St. Clare of Assisi,* by British Secular Franciscan Nesta de Robeck (d. 1983; see Oct. 1983 *The Cord*), reprinted in 1982 by Franciscan Herald Press, Chicago; *Walled in Light: Saint Colette,* by Mother Mary Francis, Poor Clare Colettine Abbess in Roswell, New Mexico (Sheed & Ward, 1959), and especially her delightful and insightful autobiographical *A Right To Be Merry* (same publisher, 1956; reprinted with a new Preface entitled "Still Merry," Franciscan Herald Press, 1973), a lively classic that merits being kept in print. Mother Mary Francis' article on "Poor Clares" in the *New Catholic Encyclopedia* provides a factual summary of their history and rules. My brief survey of all the meetings and other links between Francis and Clare appeared in *The Cord* for July, 1984. That Franciscan spiritual review (St. Bonaventure University, St. Bonaventure, New York 14778) frequently publishes studies of the spirituality of St. Clare and the Poor Clares.

Now we have two new outstanding works on that subject. *Clare: Her Light and Her Song,* by Sister Mary Seraphim of the Ohio Poor Clares of Perpetual Adoration (Franciscan Herald Press, 1984) is a full-length, well documented yet semi-fictional biography of the Saint, rich in striking spiritual insights. It favors the less strict interpretation of the still controverted enclosure problem.

Clare Among Her Sisters, by Father René-Charles Dhont, O.F.M., first appearing in French in 1973, has been translated by Sister M. Barbara and was published by the Franciscan Institute of St. Bonaventure University late in 1986. It is a study of the spirituality of St. Clare: her love for Christ, her prayer life, her ideal and practice of poverty and community, and her way of living the Gospel within the Church.

Now I would like to leave the last word of this rambling yet (I trust) informative epilogue to our great lay Franciscan mystical poet, "Brother Dante," because he penned six of the most penetrating and beautiful lines ever written on the spirit and way of life of St. Clare and her Sisters.

In the seven most mystically contemplative cantos of his *Paradiso* (cantos 21-23, 30-33), the poet masterfully outlines his concept and experience of Christian contemplation and discusses it (in his imagination) with Saints Peter Damian, Benedict, and Bernard. I would urge you to soar often into those heavenly realms with him, using one of the five readable contemporary translations: Ciardi's (Mentor), Sisson's (Regnery Gateway), Singleton's (Princeton University Press), Mandelbaum's (Bantam), or—now my favorite—Musa's (Penguin). By all means also use Father Paul Collins' splendid condensed commentary, *Pilgrim in Love: An Introduction to Dante and His Spirituality* (Loyola University Press, 1984). Regarding this book and the above-mentioned editions, see my review article in *The Cord* for November, 1985.

Dante's profoundly perceptive capsule of Poor Clare spirituality is found in the third canto of the *Paradiso* (verses 97-102), when his Poor Clare friend Piccarda Donati evokes St. Clare, without naming her:

" 'Perfect life and high merit enheaven a lady farther above,' she said to me, 'by whose Rule in your world

below they take the habit and veil in order that until they die they may watch and sleep with that Spouse who accepts every vow which Charity conforms to His pleasure.'"

That Spouse is Jesus Christ, in whose "will," as Dante wrote, "is our peace," because God's "Love moves the sun and the other stars."

It is He who speaks to us again in our times through His Poor Clare of Jerusalem, Sister Mary of the Trinity. He is the center of the mystic world of the Poor Clares, as He was of their Father St. Francis and their Mother St. Clare.

And that is their "spiritual legacy," their message, and their challenge to us. St. Clare expressed that message in this unforgettable formula in her Letter to Sister Ermentrude: "Never let the thought of Him leave your mind."

Appendix

HIDDEN GOODNESS:
Rockford's Poor Clares

Story by Robert McClory, freelance writer. Photos by Karen Engstrom, Tribune *photographer. Reprinted by permission from* Chicago Tribune Magazine, *November 6, 1983. Copyright © 1983 by* Chicago Tribune.

> *"We find that we are never more ourselves, more fulfilled, than when we deny ourselves."*
> —Abbess of the Rockford Poor Clares

The simplicity of the place is what strikes a visitor first: a cluster of brown brick buildings, very businesslike in design, attached to a chapel that is more like a small church. Behind the buildings sprawls a garden area with walkways, trees, a greenhouse, neat rows of vegetables, and a small cemetery, all 14 graves marked by headstones of identical size.

The whole nine-acre complex is enclosed by a low wall—as if to set the area apart from the noise of a nearby intersection.

A silence permeates the grounds. And as a visitor stands in the small, unadorned hall, waiting to be admitted to the visiting area, the silence seems to intensify. A soft, very courteous voice on the intercom breaks the spell: "Open the door when the buzzer sounds, walk down the hall, enter the first room on the right—and wait."

The room you enter is a parlor, with old, straight-backed wooden chairs and a window looking out on the green grounds. In one wall there is a large opening covered by a metal grate or grille. You sit and wait and the quiet gathers again—interrupted only by an occasional whisper in the distance or the gentle closing of a door.

There is a rustling in the room on the other side of the grille, and a woman's face appears. She is wearing a brown religious habit and a black veil—not starched like the sisters used to wear in the parish grammar schools and certainly not streamlined or stylized like some modern sisters prefer today—but plain and shapeless, with no pretense of fashion. She nods, smiles timidly, and motions the visitor to a chair.

The Corpus Christi Monastery of the Poor Clare Sisters sits inconspicuously on a small plot of land on the southeast side of Rockford, Illinois. The surrounding neighborhood of small homes is now a predominantly low-income community. Twenty-one [now 29] sisters ranging in age from 26 to 92 [now 18 to 95] live 24 hours a day within the monastery's walls.

The Poor Clares first came to Rockford in 1916, and they have been at the present site (formerly a private sanitarium) since 1920. They are the descendants of a Catholic religious order established 771 years ago [1212] in Italy by St. Clare, a fashionable young woman who gave up her wealth and privilege for a radical way of life as one of the early followers of St. Francis of Assisi. The order, with about 17,000 members worldwide, has changed little in the seven centuries since it was founded. Like all Catholic sisters, the Poor Clares take vows of poverty, chastity, and obedience. But in addition, they take a vow of "enclosure," committing themselves to a hidden, "cloistered" lifestyle of continuous prayer and penance.

Except for visits to a doctor or hospital they never leave the premises, even for a family wedding or the funeral of a parent. (In most Poor Clare monasteries a special "extern" sister usually does the shopping and performs other chores in the outside world.) The sisters never eat meat. They have fish once a week and on certain religious holy days. For their sustenance they depend on the food they grow and on offerings from benefactors. They go barefoot except when outside in inclement weather and wear homemade, rough-serge habits at all times, even to bed.

Each sister sleeps in a tiny cell which has only a bed with a straw mattress, a wash stand, and a chair. On her wall hang a crucifix and a crown of thorns. When she dies, the crucifix and the crown of thorns will be placed beside her before she is buried in the simple plot within the monastery walls.

The daily schedule is demanding. The community rises just after midnight to recite together in chapel a part of the divine office, the official prayer of the church—an arrangement of psalms, prayers, and other readings from the Bible. The recitation takes about 45 minutes. The sisters then meditate quietly for another half-hour before returning to their cells.

They are up again at 5 a.m. for more of the divine office and for Mass celebrated by their priest-chaplain. After breakfast—usually coffee and a piece of bread—they move to their assigned jobs: cooking, cleaning, tending the garden, making Communion wafers for Catholic churches, and sewing religious articles.

They gather again for prayers and assemble around noon for dinner, which consists of meatless soup, several vegetables, bread, and dessert. During the meal, which is eaten in silence, one of the sisters reads aloud from a theological or spiritual book. Afterwards there is a one-hour recreation period when the sisters mingle freely, chatting, laughing, and discussing their work. A few selected religious magazines and newspapers are available in the community room and library, but no secular publications are allowed. For extraordinary religious events (such as the visit of the Pope), the community borrows a television set or tunes in on the monastery's radio. But such occasions are rare.

The afternoon is spent in work and prayer. Supper at 5:30 p.m. usually consists of bread, sometimes with peanut butter or jelly, fruit, and either eggs or cheese. Then more prayer, meditation, and reading before the community members silently retire to their cells at 8:30 p.m. for three and a half hours of uninterrupted sleep before the new day begins.

From their earliest days, contemplative, cloistered orders like the Poor Clares have been something of a mystery, even to devout Catholics. They have generally been accorded the highest respect by Church authorities. Yet a life of such rigor and mortification invariably creates some uneasiness among more ordinary men and women, an uneasiness that can turn to fear and suspicion, especially in a culture that places a high value on visible achievement.

A smiling sister enters the parlor. At 50 she is a buoyant woman who looks visitors directly in the eye. When growing up in the Austin neighborhood on Chicago's West Side she bubbled over with plans and prospects. "I wanted to do so many things," she says. "I wanted to be a sister, maybe a missionary in Africa or China. And I always wanted to see the catacombs in Rome. But then I dreamt of being a nurse or, better, a doctor. And I thought about being a social worker, maybe helping root out racism from society."

In the 9th grade she talked to a priest about her enthusiasms. "He told me if I wanted to reach most people in the best way, I should think about joining a contemplative order. But I thought, no, I don't want to lock myself up. It seemed so selfish. I wanted to be normal like everyone else. Still, down deep, I knew I was kidding myself."

She moved with her family to St. Louis, and as a teenager she taught a religion class for Catholic grade-school children. The first black student had just been enrolled in the school, she recalls, and many white parents were angry. Sister remembers being especially upset at this sudden outpouring of racial animosity among churchgoing people and her own inability to change their minds. "I was on a soapbox in those days," she says, "but I saw how scarred those people were by racial hatred, how impossible it was to touch their prejudices through ordinary human interaction."

It was then that she found herself seriously pondering the power of prayer. She thought about Jesus' declaration when His disciples returned to Him disappointed because they were unable to drive a demon out of a possessed man. "That kind," said Jesus, "can only be driven out by prayer and fasting."

Perhaps it was really true, she thought, that more important and lasting things could be accomplished in a hidden life of prayer and fasting than in direct action in the world. That was the position of the contemplative religious orders she had been reading about. They seized the simple notion that all humanity is linked together in an interrelated body and that sincere prayer benefits that body as nothing else can.

So 32 years ago, when she was 18, she entered the Poor Clare monastery in Rockford. She has been off the premises only about 10 times (for medical or dental appointments). She has no hard evidence that all those years of self-denial and prayer have changed racial views in St. Louis or anywhere else. But she believes it with unshakable conviction. "I think the Lord is present in the midst of a loving community," she says, "and that love translates into a kind of power."

She pauses, trying to explain it better, make it clearer, then realizes there is no easy way to do that. "It's beautiful," she says, "how the little people understand. You know, we're constantly asked to pray for all kinds of things by all sorts of people." And indeed, the prayer requests pour in by mail and telephone—40 or 50 a week—for a variety of intentions: for world peace, for a cancer cure, for a job, for help in dealing with an alcoholic husband or wife, in thanksgiving for a healthy baby, for a reconciliation, even for a raise. Clearly these "little people" are convinced that the veiled, austere women in Rockford make a difference in the world.

In the monastery, Sister's major tasks include cleaning the halls and assisting the older nuns. She also works in food preparation and is reading some recently published books on the extraordinary value of a vegetarian diet—something Poor Clares have taken for granted for centuries.

She says she finds her simple, uncluttered life extremely satisfying. "We have no dowries, no investments, no surpluses of food or clothing. God is our security and that makes for a fulfilling existence."

"Ever since I was a girl in Appleton, Wisconsin," a young sister recalls, "I thought about serving people." By 8th grade she was convinced she had a call, a vocation, to become a sister. And she felt a special attraction to the cloistered, contemplative religious orders she had heard about. She also saw prayer and penance as fundamental kinds of service.

"My parents were always supportive," she says. "They agreed the final choice would have to be mine, but they felt I was too young to join a contemplative order." So she attended a high school run by the Sisters of St. Agnes, an active community based in Fond du Lac, Wisconsin, which specializes in teaching and hospital work. After graduation, she joined that order. She remained an active member of the Sisters of St. Agnes for 10 years, finishing her education, teaching in several schools, and working as a pastoral associate (a kind of chaplain) in a Catholic hospital in Monroe, Wisconsin. It was there that her attraction to a life of full-time prayer increased.

"I worked with the sick and suffering every day," she says. "They would always ask for prayers. And so often after an operation or crisis, someone would say, 'Sister, your prayers pulled me through.' I learned from experience how important prayer can be."

She wrote to many communities of contemplative sisters, particularly the ones that emphasize devotion to the Blessed Sacrament (the Communion bread that Catholics believe is the body of Christ). The Corpus Christi (Body of Christ) Monastery of the Poor Clares in Rockford seemed the most attractive. "Naturally, I wondered if my inclination might not represent a secret desire to flee from the outside world," she says. "But with advice from friends and the full support of my fellow sisters, I decided to give it a try. I asked myself: 'What are you afraid of? If you're running away, you'll find out soon enough and you won't stay.'"

In January of 1982, at the age of 28, Sister formally left the Sisters of St. Agnes and became a novice with the Rockford Poor Clares. Now in her second [now sixth] year of the cloistered life, she is convinced she made the right choice. "From the beginning I knew this was the place for me," she says. "This is where God wants me to spend the rest of my life."

It was not dissatisfaction with her first order that prompted the departure, she insists, "but a further call to serve people in a deeper way, to extend my apostolate as I never could in hospital work."

But, she is asked, isn't this life terribly confining for an intelligent, healthy woman?

"Not at all," she says. "You see, this is a happy house. I'm constantly impressed with how the sisters feel responsible for one another. There's a good spirit of give and take."

The seemingly archaic rules and restrictions strike Sister as altogether appropriate and "supportive of a life of prayer." The lifetime enclosure within the monastery walls, she says, is "a deep expression of the giving of self to Christ completely, a total surrender that makes you free to pray for the world." The abandonment of footwear "helps us identify with the poor and is really quite healthy." (Poor Clares reportedly have fewer foot problems than the general population.) The sharing of all things in common "reminds us that all is gift and that we are pilgrims." Never to return home, even for a parent's death, is hard, she says, "but it is a matter of choice."

She, too, searches for words to convey the ideas adequately. "Look, if someone took a job, say, in Australia, she wouldn't get home for important events, either. It's a question of choosing work you consider truly *important*."

Besides the Poor Clares, there are at least 15 other orders of Catholic religious women dedicated to the contemplative life in some 200 monasteries throughout the United States. In 1964 the Second Vatican Council said these ancient groups will "always have a distinguished part to play in Christ's Mystical Body. . . no matter how urgent may be the needs of the active apostolate. For they offer God a choice sacrifice of praise." Nevertheless, said the Council, "their manner of living should be revised according to. . . principles and standards of appropriate renewal, though their withdrawal from the world and the practices of their contemplative life should be maintained at their holiest."

Accordingly, many of these communities underwent substantial changes. The hours of the divine office (now said in the United States in English instead of Latin) were shortened; many prayers and old devotions were altered or abandoned; and some extreme forms of penance, such as protracted fasting, were eliminated. In addition, a rule was introduced requiring that all applicants pass a psychological test to determine if they are sufficiently stable for the demanding schedule and the seclusion.

The Rockford Poor Clares belong to a federation of Poor Clare monasteries which meets every three years to discuss trends and provide mutual support.

The sisters believe they are faithful in their internal organization to the reforms of the Council. "We're very much in line with the direction of religious life today," a sister remarks. "We are countercultural. We give drastic witness that God is the center of life."

Discussions of relevance are largely irrelevant to one of the elder sisters, who at 92 has been a Poor Clare for 64 years. Originally from Cleveland, she was one of those who helped establish the Rockford monastery after World War I and she has been there ever since. If extreme confinement and a life of prayer are physically or psychologically debilitating, you could not prove it by her. Sister is a tiny, alert woman with bright eyes and good hearing. She supplies quick, short answers to questions. A native of Poland, she still prays in Polish and speaks that language with close friends and relatives.

For many years she was the community's cook and chief baker. Even though old age has forced her to slow her pace, she is still a lively presence. "I've always liked work and prayer," she says. "They seem to agree with me. I think they're good for everyone."

Recently, the doctor cautioned her to pass up the community's prayers and meditation in the early morning hours—an order to which she submits out of obedience but which she doesn't particularly appreciate. "I miss it very much," she comments. "It's hard for me to get used to all this rest."

Sister says her years have been brightened by the friendly spirit of the community. "People helping people; that's what it's all about, isn't it?"

Asked for her views on the changes the church has experienced in the last 20 years, she starts to answer, then puts her hand over her mouth. "No, no, don't put that down," she says. "That's personal. That's not for the public."

The abbess of Corpus Christi Monastery does not resemble the dominant mother general who shook the rafters with "Climb Every Mountain" in the musical "The Sound of Music." She is a mild-mannered, almost shy person who nevertheless displays a firm self-confidence about herself and the community she governs. She is obviously well read, her conversation casually sprinkled with references to Catholic thinkers like Dietrich von Hildebrand, Charles de Foucauld, Jacques Maritain, and even some secular writers like E. F. Schumacher, the man who pioneered the small-is-beautiful movement.

There is a decided mystical emphasis in her outlook—a conviction that nothing is quite as it seems, that our view of reality is topsy-turvy, that the first will be last and the last first, that the meek *will* inherit the Earth. "How can you lead an easy life," she asks, "when our Lord led such a hard life?"

She does not pose the question accusingly, only as an earnest query about something that ought to be perfectly obvious to anyone who looks beneath the surface. "Our power in the Church is hidden goodness," she explains. "Just as Jesus led a hidden life, we try to do something hard for God."

But Jesus' life wasn't hidden, a visitor notes. He went around preaching, teaching, healing.

"Just for three years," she responds. "In all those 30 earlier years He was secluded, hidden away— just as He is hidden today in the Blessed Sacrament. We imitate that."

Yet all that seclusion has a mighty effect on the world, she insists, suggesting that perhaps the Eastern and Hebrew mystics of old grasped the idea most poignantly in their belief that a holy person somehow preserves the world from destruction.

In 1959, at age 20, the present abbess entered the Rockford Poor Clares after finishing two years of college in Toledo, Ohio, where she majored in psychology and chemistry. Five years ago, when she was 39, she was elected abbess by the customary majority vote of her fellow sisters. At the time she needed a dispensation from a rule that declares no one under 40 should serve as abbess.

She takes a balanced attitude toward the old-fashioned traditions of dress, diet and scheduling which the Poor Clares preserve. "I don't think we should be too hard on the old structures," she says, "nor should we get hung up on them. They're like the bottle in which the liquid is poured. The important thing is to safeguard the genuine attitude of love and sacrifice among us." Poor Clares, she predicts, will continue to hang onto the older and harder customs because "in our tradition if something is easy, we get suspicious about it."

The contemplative religious life seems strange to people today, notes the abbess, "because they are reluctant to make any commitment, to settle down. There seems to be so much restlessness. I think people are afraid to say yes. Yet we find that we are never more ourselves, never more fulfilled, than when we deny ourselves."

Her hardest job as abbess, she says, is helping sisters see that they are their own greatest penances: "We are always so blind to our faults and our goodness." She cites an example, Padre Pio, the saintly Italian monk who feared during much of his life that he was destined for damnation. "Even he needed guidance," she says.

Her greatest satisfaction, she says, is placing the Blessed Sacrament (contained in a small vessel for viewing) on the altar in the chapel every day for veneration by the sisters. This simple act she calls her "best conference and most powerful sermon" since "the Holy Eucharist extends the graces and mysteries of the Mass throughout the day and night of our life. Worship teaches us the secret of communal relationships: the joy which comes from giving a primary place to love and from trusting in God even when He seems to leave us in difficulty."

Also satisfying, she adds, is presiding over the ceremony in which each sister, on the anniversary of her official entry into religious life, kneels at the foot of the altar, places her hands in the hands of the abbess, and dedicates herself again to poverty, chastity, obedience, and enclosure. It is a ceremony

that symbolizes the function of the abbess: "supporting each member of the community in forming a
sisterhood based on the Gospel."

Some contemplative communities have been torn
by dissension and internal bickering in recent years.
Corpus Christi Monastery has enjoyed relative peace
because, as many of the sisters explain, each member depends on the group and takes responsibility
for it. Says one, "This is no place for absolute isolation, and those who come looking for it don't last
long."

The permanent population has remained stable—
at about 23—throughout most of the years. And no
one exhibits any concern for the monastery's future
prospects. For one thing, Poor Clares on principle
are not preoccupied with numbers. For another, seven
centuries of history have taught them that if they
hold to their beliefs, the community will endure and
so will their good works.

As a visitor departs, the overwhelming silence is
broken by the sound of a telephone ringing far off,
in another part of the building. More than likely
it is someone asking for prayers, some "little person" who thinks that what these sisters offer up
in their penances or sing in their chapel will have
an impact for good. There is no simple explanation
for this conviction, any more than there is a logical
rationale for the perennial attraction among women
to this hard, rigorous way of life. One man, a missionary priest from Australia, put it this way after
a week at a convention of contemplative sisters:

"One senses a realm here that reaches beyond the
horizon of human love. It is to be in touch with the
transcendent; it has something to do with the stars

and other planets—a cosmic dimension. Yes, and something more, something almost bordering on connaturality with God; of birthing and caring, of pain borne for the world."

The Poor Clares' Corpus Christi Monastery at 2111 South Main Street in Rockford, Illinois, home of some 30 sisters.

Aerial view of the Poor Clares' Corpus Christi Monastery in Rockford, Illinois. The house in the lower foreground is their chaplain's residence.

The cloister chapel where the nuns pray, especially the Liturgy of the Hours.

A close-up view of the altar in the cloister chapel. The monstrance can be seen from the Monastery's public chapel on the opposite side of this altar.

A close-up view of the main altar in the large public chapel
of the Monastery. The monstrance is also visible from the
nuns' cloister chapel just behind the main altar.

Above: The Poor Clares at prayer in their chapel. The professed sisters are wearing black veils, the novices are in white veils, and the postulants are wearing short white veils with their blue jumpers.

Below: The cross-form prayer, a centuries-old Poor Clare tradition. Each sister raises her arms in the form of a cross and silently prays five times each the Our Father, Hail Mary and Glory be, in honor of the five wounds of Our Lord.

Above: A novice praying the Liturgy of the Hours.
Below: Poor Clare nuns praying the Liturgy of the Hours.

A Poor Clare nun praying in her cell. When she dies, the crucifix on the wall will be placed in her hands and the crown of thorns will be put into the coffin by her side. A wreath of fresh white flowers will be placed on her head.

Spiritual reading is an important part of a Poor Clare's life.
The Sisters do not wear shoes except when they go outdoors.

The Sister Sacristan preparing for Mass.

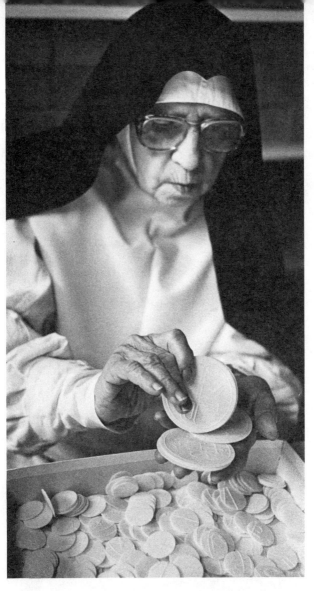

Packing hosts made by the Poor Clares.

Above: Bringing a large ladder to work on the roof. The Sisters made this cart for the ladder.
Below: Replacing a roof on one of the utility buildings.

Picking garden produce in the Monastery garden.

Above: The nuns do all their own sewing. They support themselves partly by making vestments for priests and First Communion veils for little girls.
Below: Cleaning the refectory for dinner.

Preparing meals is a daily chore joyously undertaken.

Above: Preparing food. Poor Clares maintain a vegetarian diet.
Below: Baking hosts.

Above: All work is entered into with joy.
Below: Even running the boiler is done by the nuns.

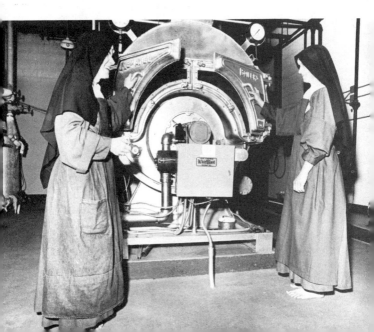

The Poor Clares at recreation, when they can visit with one another. Generally they also occupy themselves with making rosaries, sewing or some other handicraft.

The Mother Abbess greeting visitors from behind a grille.
Typical of all cloistered nuns, the Poor Clares always converse
with visitors through such a grille.

A postulant dressed as a bride—a "bride of Christ"—kneels before the altar before receiving the holy habit.

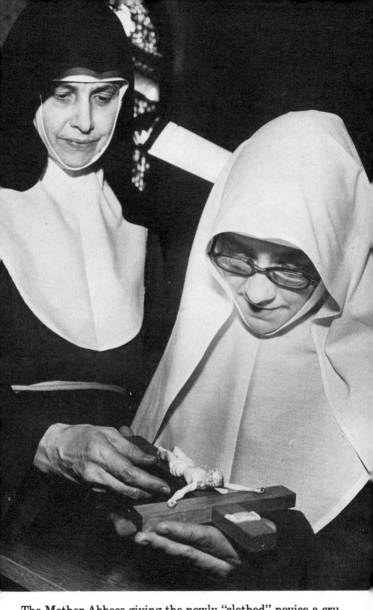

The Mother Abbess giving the newly "clothed" novice a crucifix, symbolizing the life of suffering and purgation which she is embracing.

The sisters praying in procession.

A Poor Clare nun absorbed in prayer. Prayer constitutes the principal part of her life and is the main reason she entered the Poor Clares.

A Poor Clare at night prayer before the altar—a hidden hero-
ine beseeching Our Divine Lord on behalf of suffering, mis-
guided humanity. Only in Heaven will we realize the good
done by such contemplative nuns secreted in the cloistered
monasteries of the world.

If you have enjoyed this book, consider making your next selection from among the following . . .

The Guardian Angels 2.00
Eucharistic Miracles. *Joan Carroll Cruz* 15.00
The Incorruptibles. *Joan Carroll Cruz* 13.50
Padre Pio—The Stigmatist. *Fr. Charles Carty* 15.00
Ven. Francisco Marto of Fatima. *Cirrincione*, comp. 1.50
The Facts About Luther. *Msgr. P. O'Hare*. 16.50
Little Catechism of the Curé of Ars. *St. John Vianney* 6.00
The Curé of Ars—Patron St. of Parish Priests. *O'Brien* 5.50
The Four Last Things: Death, Judgment, Hell, Heaven 7.00
Pope St. Pius X. *F. A. Forbes* 8.00
St. Alphonsus Liguori. *Frs. Miller & Aubin* 16.50
Confession of a Roman Catholic. *Paul Whitcomb*. 1.50
The Catholic Church Has the Answer. *Paul Whitcomb* 1.50
The Sinner's Guide. *Ven. Louis of Granada* 12.00
True Devotion to Mary. *St. Louis De Montfort* 8.00
Life of St. Anthony Mary Claret. *Fanchón Royer* 15.00
Autobiography of St. Anthony Mary Claret. 13.00
I Wait for You. *Sr. Josefa Menendez* 75
Words of Love. *Menendez, Betrone, Mary of the Trinity*. 6.00
Little Lives of the Great Saints. *John O'Kane Murray* 18.00
Prayer—The Key to Salvation. *Fr. Michael Müller*. 7.50
The Victories of the Martyrs. *St. Alphonsus Liguori* 10.00
Canons and Decrees of the Council of Trent. *Schroeder*. 15.00
Sermons of St. Alphonsus Liguori for Every Sunday 16.50
A Catechism of Modernism. *Fr. J. B. Lemius* 5.00
Alexandrina—The Agony and the Glory. *Johnston*. 6.00
Life of Blessed Margaret of Castello. *Fr. Bonniwell* 7.50
The Ways of Mental Prayer. *Dom Vitalis Lehodey* 14.00
Fr. Paul of Moll. *van Speybrouck* 12.50
Abortion: Yes or No? *Dr. John L. Grady, M.D.*. 2.00
The Story of the Church. *Johnson, Hannan, Dominica*. 16.50
Hell Quizzes. *Radio Replies Press* 1.50
Purgatory Quizzes. *Radio Replies Press*. 1.50
Virgin and Statue Worship Quizzes. *Radio Replies Press* 1.50
Moments Divine before/Bl. Sacr. *Reuter* 8.50
Meditation Prayer on Mary Immaculate. *Padre Pio* 1.50
Little Book of the Work of Infinite Love. *de la Touche*. 3.00
Textual Concordance of/Holy Scriptures. *Williams*. PB. 35.00
Douay-Rheims Bible. *Paperbound*. 35.00
The Way of Divine Love. (pocket, unabr.). *Menendez* 8.50
Mystical City of God—Abridged. *Ven. Mary of Agreda* 18.50

Prices subject to change.

Saint Michael and the Angels. *Approved Sources* 7.00
Dolorous Passion of Our Lord. *Anne C. Emmerich.* 16.50
Our Lady of Fatima's Peace Plan from Heaven. *Booklet.* 75
Three Ways of the Spiritual Life. *Garrigou-Lagrange* 6.00
Mystical Evolution. 2 Vols. *Fr. Arintero, O.P.* 36.00
St. Catherine Labouré of the Mirac. Medal. *Fr. Dirvin* 13.50
Manual of Practical Devotion to St. Joseph. *Patrignani* 15.00
The Active Catholic. *Fr. Palau* 7.00
Ven. Jacinta Marto of Fatima. *Cirrincione* 2.00
Reign of Christ the King. *Davies* 1.25
St. Teresa of Ávila. *William Thomas Walsh* 21.50
Isabella of Spain—The Last Crusader. *Wm. T. Walsh* 20.00
Characters of the Inquisition. *Wm. T. Walsh* 15.00
Philip II. *William Thomas Walsh.* HB. 37.50
Blood-Drenched Altars—Cath. Comment. Hist. Mexico 20.00
Self-Abandonment to Divine Providence. *de Caussade* 18.00
Way of the Cross. *Liguorian* 1.00
Way of the Cross. *Franciscan* 1.00
Modern Saints—Their Lives & Faces, Bk. 1. *Ann Ball.* 18.00
Modern Saints—Their Lives & Faces, Bk. 2. *Ann Ball.* 20.00
Divine Favors Granted to St. Joseph. *Pere Binet.* 5.00
St. Joseph Cafasso—Priest of the Gallows. *St. J. Bosco* 5.00
Catechism of the Council of Trent. *McHugh/Callan.* 24.00
Why Squander Illness? *Frs. Rumble & Carty* 2.50
Fatima—The Great Sign. *Francis Johnston* 8.00
Heliotropium—Conformity of Human Will to Divine 13.00
Charity for the Suffering Souls. *Fr. John Nageleisen* 16.50
Devotion to the Sacred Heart of Jesus. *Verheylezoon* 15.00
Sermons on Prayer. *St. Francis de Sales.* 4.00
Sermons on Our Lady. *St. Francis de Sales* 10.00
Sermons for Lent. *St. Francis de Sales.* 12.00
Fundamentals of Catholic Dogma. *Ott* 21.00
Litany of the Blessed Virgin Mary. (100 cards) 5.00
Who Is Padre Pio? *Radio Replies Press* 2.00
Child's Bible History. *Knecht.* 5.00
The Life of Christ. 4 Vols. H.B. *Anne C. Emmerich* 60.00
St. Anthony—The Wonder Worker of Padua. *Stoddard.* 5.00
The Precious Blood. *Fr. Faber* 13.50
The Holy Shroud & Four Visions. *Fr. O'Connell* 2.00
Clean Love in Courtship. *Fr. Lawrence Lovasik* 2.50
The Secret of the Rosary. *St. Louis De Montfort.* 5.00

At your Bookdealer or direct from the Publisher.
Call Toll Free 1-800-437-5876

Prices subject to change.